West Coast

Wendy Mewes

Credits

Footprint credits

Editor: Alan Murphy
Production and layout: Angus Dawson, Jen Haddington
Maps: Kevin Feeney

Managing Director: Andy Riddle
Content Director: Patrick Dawson
Publisher: Alan Murphy
Publishing Managers: Felicity Laughton, Jo Williams, Nicola Gibbs
Marketing and Partnerships Director: Liz Harper
Marketing Executive: Liz Eyles
Trade Product Manager: Diane McEntee
Account Managers: Paul Bew, Tania Ross
Advertising: Renu Sibal, Elizabeth Taylor
Finance: Phil Walsh

Photography credits

Front cover: Davidmartyn/Dreamstime
Back cover: Elena Eliseeva/Dreamstime

Printed in Great Britain by CPI Antony Rowe, Chippenham, Wiltshire

MIX
Paper from responsible sources
FSC www.fsc.org
FSC® C013604

Every effort has been made to ensure that the facts in this guidebook are accurate. However, travellers should still obtain advice from consulates, airlines, etc about travel and visa requirements before travelling. The authors and publishers cannot accept responsibility for any loss, injury or inconvenience however caused.

Publishing information

Footprint *Focus Brittany West Coast*
1st edition
© Footprint Handbooks Ltd
April 2012

ISBN: 978 1 908206 57 2
CIP DATA: A catalogue record for this book is available from the British Library

® Footprint Handbooks and the Footprint mark are a registered trademark of Footprint Handbooks Ltd

Published by Footprint
6 Riverside Court
Lower Bristol Road
Bath BA2 3DZ, UK
T +44 (0)1225 469141
F +44 (0)1225 469461
footprinttravelguides.com

Distributed in the USA by Globe Pequot Press, Guilford, Connecticut

The content of Footprint *Focus Brittany West Coast* has been extracted from Footprint's *Brittany* travel guide, which was researched and written by Wendy Mewes.

Contents

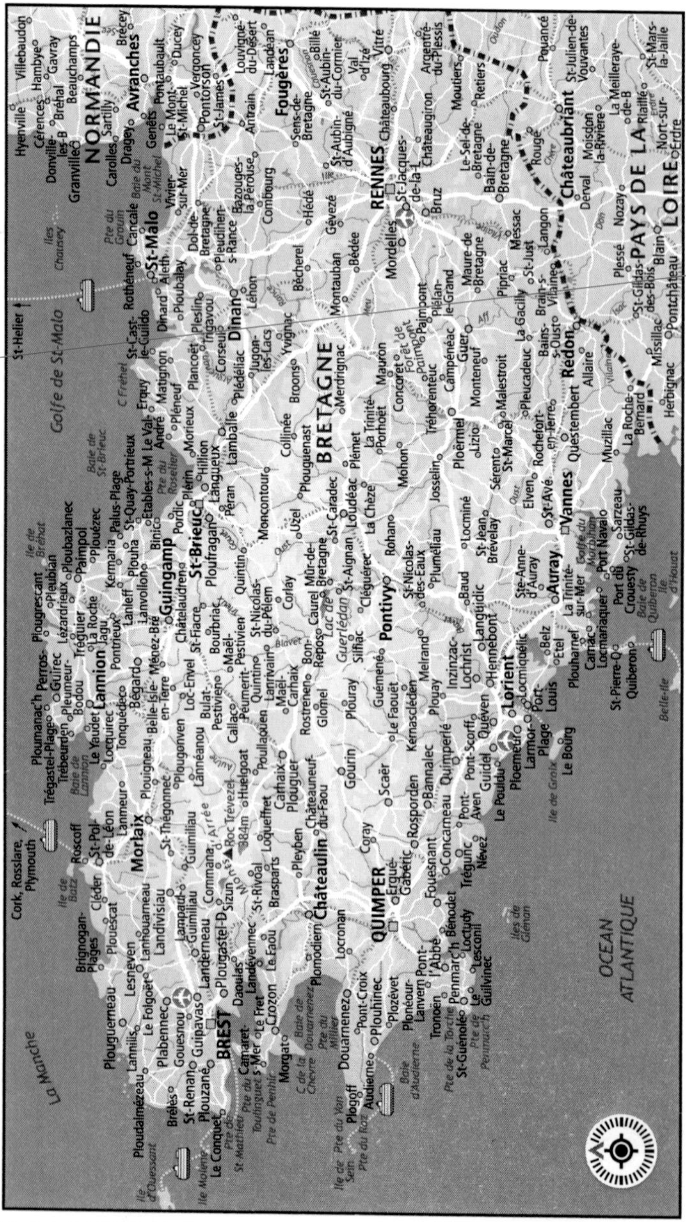
NORMANDIE
BRETAGNE
PAYS DE LA LOIRE
La Manche
Golfe de St-Malo
OCEAN ATLANTIQUE
Cork, Rosslare, Plymouth
St-Helier
BREST
QUIMPER
RENNES
Morlaix
Lannion
Guingamp
St-Brieuc
St-Malo
Dinan
Fougères
Avranches
Pontivy
Lorient
Vannes
Auray
Redon
Châteaubriant
Châteaulin
Dinard
Vitré
Belle-Île
Île de Groix
Île d'Ouessant

To visit the west of Brittany is to see this intriguing region at its most distinctively Breton: a spirited mix of vibrant traditional culture and an innovative society embracing modernity. The cities of Quimper and St-Brieuc show this in their medieval architecture and contemporary buzz, whilst post-war Brest with its powerful maritime heritage has always provided a portal to the wider world.

Celtic culture of all kinds is celebrated throughout the year in many festivals involving song, dance, local culinary traditions and colourful costumes. The Breton language, which sprang from early migrations from Great Britain when Brittany or 'Little Britain' came into existence, is still spoken in this area today.

Brittany is most famous for its magnificent coastline, especially spectacular in the west, from the wonders of the Pink Granite Coast in Côtes d'Armor to the pulsating Atlantic breakers on the wild shores of Finistère. Families in search of beach holidays and watersports lovers will find all they could desire for sandcastle-building, swimming, sailing and surfing. Walkers will enjoy the breathtaking route of the shore-hugging GR34 footpath. By contrast, this coast also retains evidence of the Second World War with the Atlantic Wall defences and memorials to the struggles of the Resistance. The fishing ports of Douarnenez and Le Guilvinec still welcome the daily catch home, reserving the marine flavour that characterizes a major fishing area, and some of the largest sailing harbours on the French Atlantic seaboard are to be found here.

The interior of this area is dominated by the Monts d'Arrée, the highest hills in Brittany, a primitive landscape of exposed schist peaks and long views, perfect for outdoor activities or megalith-hunting. Elsewhere the Argoat (land of the woods) offers a lush contrast with deep river valleys and hill-tops strewn with that Brittany trademark, the huge granite boulder.

It's hard to imagine a greater density of memorable things to see and do than in the northwest tip of France.

Planning your trip

Best time to visit West Coast Brittany

It's difficult to generalise about the weather in Brittany – it varies enormously from region to region, from coast to inland and even from one side of a hill to the other. Generally the south and east are warmer and less wet than the areas close to the Atlantic coast. Recent years have seen hot early summers in June/July, followed by wet Augusts. Water-sports and coastal activities are popular year-round, and spring and autumn are both good choices for walking and cycling holidays, with moderate temperatures and fewer visitors. Heritage sites are in business from Easter onwards, although some also have limited winter opening. Out of the main season, there are fewer accommodation options, so planning ahead is a good idea.

Places to visit in West Coast Brittany

Finistère

This westernmost department of Brittany has the best coastal variety of all, with the endless beaches and towering cliffs of the Atlantic shore. The Crozon Peninsula and Cap Sizun provide the finest sea views, walking and water-based activities that anyone could wish for. Northwest of Brest is the westernmost point of France at Pointe de Corsen, and also the tallest standing menhir in France near St-Renan. Brest itself is essentially a modern university city, but there's plenty of interest with three port areas and the well-preserved château housing a maritime museum.

In the south of the department, Quimper could not be more different – compact and bright, with a really enjoyable medieval centre of ultra-modern shops and a breathtaking cathedral. The town of Pont l'Abbé just to the south is the heart of Pays Bigouden, a distinctive area with a long maritime history and still strong on Breton traditions today.

In the centre of Finistère, the Monts d'Arrée are the highest hills in Brittany. They're hardly mountains, but look impressive in the range of lonely schist peaks and empty moorland, set around the bowl of a reservoir and topped by the tiny chapel of St-Michel. There is plenty of scope for cultural or activity holidays in this extremely quiet area, which deserves to be better known, not only for its landscape but also as the home of some of the earliest established eco-museums in France. Just to the north is the old town of Morlaix, sacked by the English in 1522, but now more peaceably the first stop for those off the ferry at Roscoff. The ancient centre has some extraordinary old houses that you won't see elsewhere, and delightful twisting stepped passageways wiggling across the hillsides. Easily accessible from here are the *enclos paroissiaux* (parish closes), a phenomenon of religious architecture that draws visitors from afar. St-Thégonnec, Guimiliau and Lampaul-Guimiliau are close enough to visit in succession. Most of central Finistère is part of the regional Parc Naturel d'Armorique.

Côtes d'Armor

This department was called Côtes du Nord until the 1990s when it was deemed necessary to shed a rather wintry image. Armor, the land of the sea, has a stunning northern coastline, with its craggy cliffs – the highest in Brittany near Plouha and the most exotic along the Pink Granite coast around Perros-Guirec, where the fantastically shaped

Best of West Coast Brittany

Cathedral of St-Corentin, Quimper According to legend, King Gradlon called on St-Corentin to be the first bishop of Quimper in the fifth century. Building of the current cathedral started in 1239 but was delayed by the turbulence of war and plague in the 14th century. On resumption, the nave was added at a crooked angle, an oddity which only enhances the radiance of the interior today. Page 29.

Menhir de Kerloas This is the tallest upright standing stone in France, at almost 11 m. Legend said that hidden treasure beneath the menhir was revealed when the stone went off to drink from the ocean on the first stroke of midnight on Christmas Eve. However, since it returned on the second stroke, no one ever had time to get rich and stay alive. Page 39.

Camaret One of the most attractive ports in Brittany, Camaret has a long fishing tradition and a reputation as the place for lobsters. At the end of the natural curving cob is the glowing Tour Vauban, which fought off an English attack in 1694. Brightly painted houses, swimming beaches and superb coastal walks along the cliff paths add to the attraction. Page 45.

Morlaix This fascinating town, long a trading contact and rival of England, is often overlooked by tourists getting off the ferry at Roscoff and whizzing past on their way south. The ancient centre is dominated by the towering granite viaduct which brought the Paris–Brest railway line in the 1860s. Don't miss the unique architectural form of the maisons à pondalez. Page 55.

Monts d'Arrée These 'mountains' are in fact the highest hills in Brittany. The bleak moors and craggy peaks often rise out of waves of thick mist over the basin of the reservoir at the heart of the Amorican regional park. Beware the black dog roaming the marshes at night! The mystical atmosphere is heightened by the little chapel of St-Michel, a lone sentinel on its hilltop. Page 56.

Côte de Goëlo With the highest cliffs in Brittany near Plouha, glorious beaches, secluded coves and a series of pretty ports, this stretch of coastline has everything to offer for a family holiday or for those interested in outdoor activities. Following the coastal path along the green heights provides panoramic views and seascapes in the Bay of St-Brieuc. Page 65.

Tréguier cathedral This glorious cathedral contains the tomb of St-Yves, patron saint of Brittany, a lawyer famous for his impartial treatment of both rich and poor. Lawyers from all over the world attend the Pardon of St-Yves in May each year, when the relic of his skull is taken in procession to Minihy where he was born in 1250. Page 74.

Pink Granite Coast Weird and wonderful best describes the remarkable rock formations along this section of the northern coast, and the glowing pink of the granite only adds to the spectacle. Names like The Tortoise and Napoleon's Hat give an idea of what to expect, but it's the sheer size and scale of this geological wonder that's dazzling. Page 74.

rock formations draw visitors from all over the world. Boat trips to the Sept Iles bird reserve and the popular Ile de Bréhat are further attractions. In summer this whole area is packed with people and, inevitably, cars. The Côte de Goëlo offers many sandy beaches, cliff-top walks and friendly traditional family resorts like Binic and Saint-Quay Portrieux.

The only large town of Côtes d'Armor is St-Brieuc, buried deep in a double valley below the motorway flyover. It has a small medieval quarter, dominated by the somewhat prison-like Cathedral of St-Etienne and a port area down at Le Légué. Lannion Is a rather more lively and engaging town, and Tréguier, centre of the Trégor region, is a real gem of a place. Both these towns have strong visual appeal, with bright half-timbered houses and some exceptional religious architecture. Tréguier's cathedral is the finest example.

Inland, there are no big towns, and it is much less densely populated than the coastal area, with rocky or wooded undulating countryside, called the Argoat (Land of the Woods), granite villages, isolated chapels and many Neolithic standing stones or burial places.

Getting to West Coast Brittany

Air

From UK and Ireland Two budget airlines connect the UK to Brittany. You can fly to **Dinard** airport (near **St-Malo**) from the East Midlands or Stansted with **Ryanair** (ryanair.com). Prices are from €30 one way. Dinard airport is at Pleurtuit, and does not have a shuttle service, so taxis will be necessary to get to the nearest big centre at St-Malo (9 km/allow €20).

Flybe (flybe.com) has budget flights into **Rennes** airport from Southampton, Manchester, Leeds, Edinburgh, Glasgow and Belfast, from €50 one way. The airport is 20 minutes by bus (No 57) from the centre.

Flybe also has flights to **Brest** (Guipavas), although Ryanair has withdrawn this route at the time of writing. From here a bus shuttle service (€4.60 single, €8.40 return) goes to the city centre and station. These cheap flights are not year round and are liable to change, so check websites for details.

AerLingus (aerlingus.com) flies from Dublin to **Rennes** and **Aer Arann** (aerarann.com) from Ireland to **Lorient** and **Brest** (not all year round).

Air France (airfrance.fr) provides a regular service to Paris and also flies from Paris (Charles de Gaulle airport) to the regional airports of **Rennes**, **Brest**, **Lorient**, **Lannion** and **Quimper**.

From North America There are flights to Paris with Air France, British Airways, Delta; then go via Air France to regional airports, or take the train to the major towns around Brittany.

Airport information Dinard airport (T02 99 46 18 46, dinard.aeroport.fr, and good information from the unofficial site dinardairport.net); **Brest airport** (T02 98 32 86 00, or T02 98 32 86 37 for parking info, brest.aeroport.fr); **Rennes airport** (T02 99 29 60 00, rennes.aeroport.fr); **Lorient airport** (lorient-aeroport.fr).

Car-hire facilities are available at all the airports, with local details on the airport websites. The companies with offices in major towns are **Hertz** (hertz.com.fr), **Avis** (avis.fr), **Europcar** (europcar.fr) and **Sixt** (sixt.fr).

Rail

You can travel by **Eurostar** from St Pancras to Paris, Gare du Nord in 2½ hours, and then continue by high-speed TGV from Gare Montparnasse to all the major towns in Brittany

(Rennes two hours, Brest and Quimper four hours). Changing from the Eurostar at Lille and proceeding direct to Rennes is easier, avoiding the station change in Paris.

European Rail (europeanrail.com) and **Rail Europe** (raileurope.co.uk) have details of timetables, fares and ticket booking. Discount passes are available for young people and senior citizens.

For timetabling information within France, see the rail network **SNCF** site, voyages-sncf.fr.

Road

Bus **Eurolines** (eurolines.co.uk) and Europe Bus (europebus.co.uk) provide coach services to Rennes.

Car Driving from the Channel ports will take up to seven hours from Calais and about three hours from Caen and Cherbourg. Allow three hours from Paris to Rennes (348 km), or five hours to go on to Brest (593 km). There are no motorway tolls once you get into Brittany.

Michelin (viamichelin.com) are the standard road maps and they have a route-planning service.

You must have a valid driving licence, car registration documents, insurance and a nationality plate.

Sea

Direct ferries to Brittany are run only by **Brittany Ferries** (brittanyferries.com), with sailings to St-Malo from Portsmouth (9-10 hours, usually overnight from England), or from Plymouth to Roscoff (six to eight hours). There is also a service from Cork in Ireland to Roscoff. The website has a timetable and prices, but these do vary according to how far in advance you buy a ticket. Off-season schedules are published only briefly in advance and there are usually no ferries in January.

This monopoly makes fares expensive, so an alternative route is to cross the eastern end of the Channel or to Cherbourg and then drive. This takes about seven hours from Calais, 4½ hours from Dieppe and three hours from Caen or Cherbourg, but there will be the added cost of motorways tolls and petrol, so weighing up the benefits is an exercise in precision. The relatively easy access of Plymouth by motorway in the UK, avoiding the southeast, could also be a factor in opting for the Roscoff route.

Other cross-channel ferry companies are **P&O** (poferries.com), **Condor** (condorferries.com), **Speed Ferries** (speedferry.co.uk) and **LD Lines** (ldlines.co.uk). **Ferrysavers.co.uk** is worth a look for getting the best deal, as there are many permutations according to season and choice of crossing ports. **Irish Ferries** (irishferries.com) sail from Rosslare to Roscoff and Cherbourg.

Transport in West Coast Brittany

Rail

The state rail network **SNCF** has a good TGV (high-speed) service within Brittany connecting the main towns. The northern route goes through Dinan, St-Brieuc, Guingamp and Morlaix to Brest. Rennes has a link with Quimper, or there's a southern route via Nantes to Vannes and Quimper. You can check routes, timetables and price options or book tickets on voyages-sncf.fr.

Within the region, the **TER** network (ter-sncf.com/Bretagne) connects coastal spots including St-Malo, Roscoff and Quiberon and important towns such as Pontivy and Carhaix-Plouguer, but in general rural central Brittany is not well served by public transport. Use the search facility on the website for details of the KorriGo card, which can be used on regional trains, and other public transport networks.

When travelling around, you must validate (*composter*) your train ticket at the orange machine on the platform before getting on board.

Various discount schemes are available from SNCF, including the 'Carte 12-25 ans' for young people, and the over 60s 'Tarif Découverte'. Some restrictions of travel may apply. To view facilities for disabled passengers, see the Mobilité Réduite information on voyages-sncf.fr.

Bicycles can only go on certain trains – check for the symbol on timetables or ask before booking.

Finistère Trains link Brest with Morlaix, Quimper and Paris. The TGV from Paris to Brest via Morlaix takes 4½ hours. Details on voyages-sncf.fr.

Côtes d'Armor The Paris–Brest TGV line has main stations at Lamballe, St-Brieuc and Guingamp. For times and fares, see voyages-sncf.com.

There are local lines from Guingamp to Paimpol (45 minutes) and Lannion (35 minutes), and from Lamballe to Dinan (35 minutes). For details, see ter-sncf.com/bretagne.

Road

Bicycle The main towns have cycle lanes. Rennes has a bike (*vélo*) scheme whereby you can pick up a bicycle from one of the special ranks and drop it off at another elsewhere in the town. The bikes have baskets and some have child seats. Rental times vary from an hour to a day or a week, but advanced registration and a large deposit are needed. The tourist office has details, or see levelostar.fr (**Rennes**). Brest is probably the least cycle-friendly of the large centres, and this won't be helped by the new tramway system.

Most towns of any size, and places in the coastal holiday areas, have bike hire from cycle shops or camping sites. Tourist offices will have details. There's a useful list of providers near Green Ways at randobreizh.com. The largely car-free islands have bike hire near the arrival port.

Bus/coach

Each district has its own transport network, with urban and rural routes. The system is reliable and efficient, although the countryside is not especially well served. More buses cover coastal routes in summer when demand is high. The local bus station (*gare routière*) will have information, and there are special offices to provide help in big towns.

Finistère (Brest: T02 98 80 30 30, bibus.fr, Quimper: T02 98 95 26 27, qub.fr). For journeys further afield, check viaoo29.fr. A standard fare of €2 operates on most routes.

Côtes d'Armor (tibus.fr). St-Brieuc is at the hub of the Tibus network – for a plan and timetables consult the website. A single journey ticket is €2, or €40 for a monthly card.

More buses serve the coastal resorts in summer. There are three daily services from Lannion to Paimpol (about one hour), via Tréguier, and Line 15 will take you all around the Pink Granite Coast.

Car

Driving in Brittany is a pleasure, with generally good roads, no expressway tolls and comparatively little traffic. You must give way to traffic from the right at junctions, unless otherwise indicated. It is not often the case in the countryside, but be extra vigilant in towns.

From Roscoff or St-Malo, the rest of Brittany is easily accessible via express routes – N12 in the north (Brest, Morlaix, St-Brieuc), N164 in the centre (Carhaix-Plouguer to Rennes, still with some single-lane sections) and N165 in the south (Quimper, Lorient, Vannes). Rennes is at the hub of the major routes.

Parking Parking is usually pay and display in central town areas, and you must get a ticket from the machine (*horodateur*). Be especially careful not to park overnight in squares where markets are held early the following morning. Blue-lined parking bays mean you must buy a limited time disc from a presse/tabac. These are useful if you're spending several days in one place.

If you are planning on staying a while in Rennes or Brest it makes sense to use the huge central underground paying car parks. Even several days' secure parking will come to little more than €25, and the machine will take credit cards.

Regulations Police can impose on-the-spot fines for offences, such as not stopping properly at a stop sign or running a red light. Pay strict attention to drinking and driving regulations (0.5g/L) and speed limits – patrols and testing are common.

You must carry a red warning triangle and at least one reflective safety jacket – this is obligatory. Don't forget that you must have your headlight beam adjusted to the right, or buy special stickers to achieve the same effect.

Maps The best maps are **Michelin** (michelin.com). **IGN** (ign.fr) have orange departmental driving maps, but these do not mark places of interest. Their blue topographical Cartes de Randonnée with walking routes marked are useful for driving on smaller roads and worth buying if you are based in one particular area.

Where to stay in West Coast Brittany

Brittany has a good range of accommodation – hotels, B&Bs/*chambres d'hôtes, chambres chez l'habitant*, gîtes and campsites can all be found in most areas. There is a much greater choice in the summer season, however, and many establishments in all those categories are closed for up to six months of the year. It's not difficult to find a historic building to stay in as more and more manoirs offer *chambres d'hôtes* or *gîtes* in converted outbuildings. If you'd like something a bit different, some campsites now offer yurts or restored gipsy caravans. If you're planning a walking or other activity holiday outside June to September, it is best to get organized and book in advance as the limited accommodation available can get filled up quickly. Similarly, if you're looking for something on the coast in high season you'll need to book early for the best places.

Booking

It is always advisable to book in advance, but between June and September you should have little difficulty finding something on the spot as long as you are prepared to travel a little inland from the coast. Many hotels offer online booking, but it is always worth phoning for special deals and offers, especially for families.

Tourist offices will have lists of rooms available according to your criteria, and some actually book places for you. If travelling in the summer months, booking in advance is sensible, especially if you want a good coastal spot. Single-night bookings may be refused in July and August in B&Bs and some hotels.

Costs

Accommodation is more expensive on the coast and in large towns, but overall prices are generally cheap. You can expect to pay between €55 and €90 for a double room, and even the most luxurious hotel is unlikely to take you over the €200 mark. A sea view or balcony/terrace will add a few euros to the tariff. Prices are highest in July and August, with mid-season from May to June and September. Low season is in autumn/winter and often excludes Christmas to New Year.

In hotels, breakfast is not included in the price of the room and this can be a significant extra cost, from €7 up to €15 per person. It may be worth refusing the option and going to a nearby bar for coffee, picking up fresh croissants from a bakery on the way. On the other hand, a lavish hotel buffet breakfast can keep you going all day. The B&B/*chambres d'hôtes* room tariff nearly always includes breakfast, which consists at the most basic of bread and jam, with possible additions of cereal and croissants. Expect to pay €45-75 for an en suite room. Rooms *chez l'habitant*, where you may have to share a bathroom or toilet, are likely to be cheaper.

A local *taxe de séjour* (usually €0.5-1.50), which goes to the municipality towards infrastructures relevant to tourism, may be added to the bill in hotels, furnished rooms and on campsites. It is applied per adult per night in season (and not extended to children).

Hotels

A huge variety of hotels is available, from château-style or spa luxury with all the facilities and gourmet dining, down to the simple country *auberge* with a few rooms above the bar. The star grading system is from one to five – anything with two stars should be more than adequate, with TV and a small desk/table area in the room and often toiletries and hairdryers in the bathrooms, which are often shower only. Wi-Fi is found in many hotels.

Individuals should look out for the offer of a *soirée étape* (sometimes only for business customers) – you pay a single price for room, dinner and breakfast and it's usually a real bargain. Hotels without a restaurant often offer this in conjunction with a local place to eat. A hotel with a restaurant offering *demi-pension* usually has a good-value evening menu for residents only, rather than dining à la carte.

Hotel chains include the ubiquitous Logis de France (independent hotels conforming to a quality standard that is usually reliable), but there is quite a variation in terms of ambience and individuality. For budget holidays there are more options these days with the likes of B&B, Etap and Formule 1. These are essentially motels, with, for example, limited reception hours (automated opening facilities otherwise), drinks machines and basic meal dispensers. Rooms are usually adequate, if on the small side, and better for the odd night when travelling than for a week's relaxing break. If it's comfort you're after, the top end of the price range includes Oceania, Best Western and Kyriad chains.

Tipping is appreciated but not expected in hotels.

B&B/Chambres d'hôtes

The quality of *chambres d'hôtes* is naturally variable, but you can usually expect a private or en suite bath or shower room and toilet. There may also be a guest lounge. Furniture and furnishings vary greatly, with comfortable chairs, writing tables and televisions not

Price codes

Where to stay

€€€€ over €200	€€€ €100-200
€€ €60-100	€ under €60

Prices refer to the cost of two people sharing a double room in the high season.

Restaurants

€€€€ over €40	€€€ €30-40
€€ €20-30	€ under €20

Prices refer to the average cost of a two-course meal for one person, with a drink and service and cover charge.

necessarily as standard. Tea/coffee-making facilities are not common, except in British-run places. Wi-Fi is sometimes, but not often, available in B&Bs. If the size of a room or a particular facility is important to you, do ask specifically when booking. Note that it may be necessary to share facilities such as a bathroom in a room *chez l'habitant*. If establishments offer tables d'hôtes, you eat the evening meal with the family, but this is only usually a service if there are no restaurants in the vicinity (a rare case) or if the proprietor is a passionate cook. Breakfast may include local or home-made products. Many B&Bs offer a corner kitchen where guests can prepare simple meals in the evening (and the use of the garden for eating outside). Hosts generally do not expect full-scale cooking to take place here.

As far as quality marks go, *Clévacances* is a recognized label for B&Bs (up to five letting rooms), with a system of keys from one to four, reflecting the comfort and amenities of each room.

More and more B&Bs do not take single-night bookings in the summer months.

Bienvenue à la ferme (bretagnealaferme.com) is an organization assuring standards for accommodation on working farms, where the whole rural experience is part of the package. (As well as *chambres d'hôtes*, this may include camping and *gîtes*.) Often walking routes are offered or riding organized, and farm produce will be available, as well as visits to see the animals.

Accueil Paysan Bretagne (accueil-paysan-bretagne.com) is a similar network with accommodation in authentic rural working households, where food and/or drink are often produced on the premises.

Self-catering

Self-catering options include gîtes (which are often run by British owners these days) and caravan/chalet rentals on the numerous campsites. The latter is a useful aid for walkers on long-distance paths outside of the summer months (when single-night bookings may be refused). A gîte may be next to the owner's home, on a farm, in a complex of converted outbuildings or a single cottage on its own. The *gîte rural*, as the name suggests, is out in the countryside.

Gîtes usually have well-equipped kitchens, sitting areas, TVs and local tourist information for you to make the most of your stay. Outdoor space will have garden furniture and often a BBQ. Washing machines/dishwashers are common, but ask beforehand if they are essentials for you. Expect to pay from €500-1000 for a week in high season.

Gîtes de France (gites-de-france.com) has thousands of graded properties throughout

Brittany. There is also the *Clévacances* quality mark, using keys (one to four for studios and apartments, one to five for gîtes). The *Clef Verte* (green key) scheme is a rare award for ecological quality.

A *gîte d'étape* is a hostel with basic accommodation for walkers, cyclists and riders who are journeying around and looking for a cheap night's stay. Facilities vary, but there'll be a kitchen, dormitory (sometimes single/double rooms too) and shared bathrooms. Usually breakfast and packed lunches will be available, and maybe an evening meal if booked in advance. The *Rando Accueil* (rando-accueil.com) mark should guarantee knowledgeable hosts and good standards of accommodation.

Youth hostels (*auberges de jeunesse*) are another good bet for cheap accommodation (see aubergesdejeunesse.com), and are not only open to young people. There's a Pass Bretagne that offers a sixth night free after getting five stamps from different establishments in the scheme.

Another increasingly popular choice is to rent an apartment or studio in a Résidence building, frequently situated in a town or by the coast. This is a compromise between hotels and self-catering, with different levels of extra services, from babysitting to provision of meals. Room size varies considerably, so check in advance to avoid disappointment on arrival. Many residences have organized outings and entertainment in the summer months, and some include restaurant or bar services then too. Kitchens will be fully equipped if you prefer to cook for yourself. Many offer baby equipment, down to the last dummy and even a pushchair, to save bringing everything with you.

Camping

There are numerous campsites in Brittany, mostly on the coast but also often by rivers. Many small towns and villages have municipal sites, open only from June to September and good value for basic amenities. Larger commercial sites have caravans, chalets and mobile homes (or even yurts occasionally) to rent by the week, but out of high season you can also find these useful for an overnight stop. Cabins in the trees are the latest thing, and more sites are now offering them.

Arranged activities for children are another advantage for this type of well-organized accommodation. Larger sites will also have some sort of shop and a swimming pool. Few sites are open all year round, but March to October is getting more common. The typical cost is €15-25 a night for pitch, car and two people, plus a few euros extra for children, pets, electricity and so on.

Food and drink in West Coast Brittany

Brittany is a cheap place to eat and you will never be far from a restaurant or crêperie where you can get a meal for less than €20. Lunch begins at midday, when a great flock of white vans descend on the little restaurants offering the best *ouvrières* deals, a meal with drinks for about €11. In towns many office workers regularly eat lunch out, so restaurants can be crowded. It is not so common to dine out in the evening, except in large towns, but popular places will be busy from 2000 onwards. The good news is that it's rare to find a service charge here, and tipping is not expected in a regular way, although rounding up the bill is a nice gesture if you are satisfied.

Crêpes and galettes

Brittany has a tradition of peasant cooking – cheap, filling dishes, easily prepared over cottage fires. Crêpes and *galettes* (pancakes) are ubiquitous now, with many different recipes and textures according to different regions or even villages. The Breton-speaking western part of the region uses the term crêpes (being most like the Breton *krampouz*), while galettes for the savoury version is more common in eastern Brittany. The use of *blé noir* (buckwheat) flour is traditional for savoury fillings. This is the basic Breton flour, historically important because it grew well and quickly in poor soil. Froment or white flour is mostly used for dessert crêpes.

Many people eat several crêpes at a sitting. If you visit a Breton home, be prepared to start with a plain buttered dark pancake, move on to a few with meat and eggs and then get set in for the jam and fruit delights. Don't count, just eat! In the markets you can buy freshly made crêpes and marvel at the dexterous skill of the cook. The traditional fillings are basic farm staples – ham, bacon, sausage, eggs – and then there are all manner of fishy options such as scallops, smoked salmon or even sardines. Desserts mostly centre around apples and pears, chocolate and caramel, honey and jam, with flambéed versions too. If you don't like the commercial whipped cream that sometimes swamps these, ask for your crêpe '*sans chantilly*'. In most crêperies you can choose your own combination of ingredients from a list. Like everything else, the crêpe has developed, and modern attempts at originality may produce extraordinary options like fig and foie gras. Occasionally crêpes come with a green salad or you can ask for one, but otherwise there is no garnish, and no bread is served with the meal. Main course salads are usually on offer in crêperies too, and sometimes omelettes.

If you want to try creating a crêpe meal in your self-catering accommodation, you can buy fresh crêpes from many bakeries or in packets (hand or machine made) from supermarkets.

Fish and shellfish

Fish is the other staple of the Breton diet in this major fishing area of France. Shellfish (*fruits de mer*) is the thing to try, with vast arrays piled on huge plates, especially in restaurants around the coast. Dining rooms are often filled with the sound of cracking, clattering and slurping – at one Brest restaurant you just get a board with a crab and a mallet. *Coquilles St-Jacques* (scallops) are the speciality of the region (and the symbol of the Santiago de Compostela pilgrimage trail), and the best are to be found in the Bays of St-Brieuc and Morlaix in the north, and Concarneau in the south. You will find them served with and without the orange-coloured part of the coral, and the simplest cooking – generally pan-fried in a little butter – is the best way to appreciate the flavour. Another common offering is mussels, and you'll find *moules frites* (mussels with fries) everywhere, or *moules à la marinière*, with a thin white wine liquor. Other popular sauces for mussels include cream and curry. Mussels are often grown on stakes (*bouchots*) or lines of ropes, which you can see in coastal areas. Moules of the Baie de St-Michel were the first to be given an AOC (*appellation d'origine contrôlée*), a guarantee of quality and origin.

Contrary to the popular saying, it is possible to eat oysters (*huîtres*) in months without an 'r' in them, the traditional reproductive time. Oysters are produced in various ways, but the most sought-after is the flat Belon oyster from Finistère, at their best from September. The combination of fresh and salted water produces a fine flavour, usually likened to that of hazelnut. Deep-sea oysters are to be found around Paimpol.

Lobster (*homard*) is also popular, including the special deep-water homard Breton, which is blue in colour. Restaurants oftesn offer *homard l'armoricain*, lobster with a sauce of shallots, garlic, white wine, tomatoes and a hint of chilli.

Langoustines can be found in most coastal towns, as well as shrimps (*crevettes*) and prawns, spider crabs and rock crabs caught in pots like lobsters. At low tide you will see people out collecting *huîtres sauvages*, rock crabs, clams, cockles and all manner of other small shellfish from the rocks. There are restrictions on the sizes that can be taken and, if you decide to try yourself, you must replace any stone or rock so as not to disturb the natural ecological balance (and be sure you know the tide times).

Cotriade is a substantial fish soup with vegetables and potatoes, the name coming from the *Kaoter* cooking pot, but a general soupe du poisson made with whatever is available is commonly offered in coastal places. It usually comes with croutons, cheese and spicy rouille paste. Sardines are a staple catch and almost a historical symbol of Pays Bigouden; do try them freshly grilled at a port restaurant there. Brittany has always been at the forefront of the food conserving industry, and especially preserved fish, which is particularly successful for oily species such as sardine, mackerel and tuna. *Rillettes* are a sort of pâté of mashed flesh with oil and seasonings, which makes a perfect sauce for pasta with a little thinning down, or a starter with bread. Smoked fish – mainly sardine, mackerel or trout – is also worth looking out for, whether from traditional smokehouses or simply hung up in a chimney. Tinned fish products, often preserved in a muscadet-based liquid, are perfect for picnics – you need nothing more than a rough country bread to dip.

The commonest white fish served in restaurants are *lieu jaune* (pollack), *cabillaud* (cod), *merlu* (hake) and *anglefin* (haddock), but if you get the chance, try the prized and delicate *bar* (sea bass) and *daurade* (bream). Red mullet (*rouget*) is also a treat, often served en cocotte, in a small casserole. Fresh-water fish include trout (*truite*) and salmon (*saumon*).

If you're self-catering, try to buy from a market or specialist *poissonnerie*, although good-quality fish is also available from supermarkets. At ports you can be sure of an extra-fresh catch just off the boats in the morning or evening. The *criée* is the name for the auction held when the boats return, and at certain ports the public can attend the sale – it is part of some visits at Haliotika, the centre of discovery for the fishing industry at Le Guilvinec in Finistere.

Brittany has more than 600 varieties of seaweed (generally called *algues*) and, although they are not all edible, their use in cooking is increasingly popular. The flavour can be strong and *algues* should be used sparingly, but well-cooked as an accompaniment to fish or in omelettes and crêpes, it's delicious. The salty sea vegetable samphire also appears on menus, sometimes a bit on the vinegary side, but tasty when pan-fried with a hint of garlic.

Meat and vegetables

Pork, chicken and turkey are all commonly available on menus, as well as steak, either entrecôte or *faux-filet* (sirloin). Lamb is a traditional Breton meat, with those from Belle-Ile particularly well known for their flavour. Ask for meat *sanglant* (rare), *à point* (medium) or *bien cuit* (well done). Plats du terroir on a menu indicate tasty locally sourced ingredients.

There are many excellent cold meats (*charcuterie*) for sandwiches and to accompany salads. The local *traiteur*, who offers ready-prepared delicatessen dishes, will have a whole range of suitable picnic foods. The famous *andouille* sausage, a Breton speciality, with the best coming from Guéméné-sur-Scorff in Morbihan, is made from cows' intestines and has an intense, rich flavour. Thin slices are often used as a filling for crêpes. There is even a festival in its honour!

Another favourite with locals in western Brittany is *Kig ar Farz* (meat and stuffing), essentially a collection of boiled meats (pork, bacon, sausage) with cabbage or other vegetables, and buckwheat flour stuffing that has been cooked in a bag, in with the rest of the ingredients. You need a large appetite to work your way through this often stodgy speciality.

Brittany is also one of the most prolific vegetable-growing areas in France, especially Léon, northern Finistère. Brittany Ferries began life as a means of transporting vegetables to Cornish markets, and artichokes have long been flown to Paris and New York to supply top restaurants. Eating the artichoke is a time-consuming and fiddly occupation of peeling, sucking and dipping the fleshy based leaves.

Cauliflowers and the *oignon rosé* (pink onion) of Roscoff are the other bumper crops. Onion-sellers or Johnnies used to travel across the channel with their bikes and strings of onions to sell to UK housewives door to door: there is a museum of their history in Roscoff. The Coco de Paimpol, a small white bean from northern Côtes d'Armor (brought from South America early in the 20th century), is often found in restaurants, usually in conjunction with white-fleshed fish.

Fruit and nuts

Fruits tend to do best in the milder, drier southeast, but the strawberries of Plougastel in Finistère are famous worldwide, so try them fresh or in delicious jam. More exotically, Le Petit Gris de Rennes is a small flavoursome melon grown around the capital. Apples for cider-making and traditional cakes are the major fruit crop, especially in the valley of the Rance around Dinan, and Pays Bigouden in southern Finistère.

Chestnuts have always been prized for their nutritional value in a poor diet, and bread or savoury cake made from chestnut flour is delicious. The Redon area in eastern Brittany is famous for their use In the Frigousse stew. Each October there is a festival in the town celebrating the chestnut. Travelling round the countryside you'll see many hamlets called Quistinic, which means a place of chestnuts in Breton.

Dairy

While cheese is not an established regional product for Brittany, there are many first-rate producers of organic goat's cheese to be found around the area, especially at regular markets. The monks at Timadeuc Abbey in Morbihan also produce a good cheese called Trappe.

Dairy products are generally excellent – salted butter has always been a vital part of the Breton diet, so important that it figures in religious rituals, such as the Pardon du Beurre at Notre-Dame de Crann at Spezet, with its butter sculptures. In the eastern part of historic Brittany, the salt-marshes, especially around Guérande, provided the perfect addition. Buttermilk (*lait ribot*) is also widely available and used in cooking.

Desserts and cakes

The traditional Breton dessert is the *far*, available on many menus and in almost every bakery (*boulangerie*). It is a solid custard flan of variable texture, sometimes plain, sometimes with prunes or other fruit for novelty value. The no-nonsense named *flan* is a cheap, often tasteless version.

The cake to try before all others is *kouign amann*, a round, dense product made from multiply folded bread dough, sugar and salted butter; very rich and satisfying. The real thing needs no addition, but you do sometimes see apple versions. The commonly found *gâteau Breton* has a hard exterior, a round form and very dense texture, and often a thin layer of jam-like filling, perhaps raspberry or prune.

Brittany is famous for its butter biscuits, a cheap and delicious souvenir to take home. The best are *palets*, thick circles that crumble in the mouth, and *galettes*, a thin, crunchier form. *Crêpes dentelles* are crispy biscuits in the form of a rolled crêpe, a speciality of Quimper, often served with ice cream.

Drinks

Cider is the staple drink to accompany crêpes and you will find little pottery cups (*bolées*) on the tables of most crêperies. You can buy a small jug (*pichet*) if you think a whole bottle may be too much. Cider is eligible for an AOC (Appellation d'Origine Contrôlée) and the best brands come from Pays Bigouden in Finistère and the Valley of the Rance near Dinan. Try to look for reputable makes such as Kerne (Pays Bigouden) or Cidre Val du Rance, or the AOC/ *Fermier* label to avoid the industrial products on many supermarket shelves. And when out and about, try a Breton kir, made with cider (instead of white wine) and the usual cassis.

Different areas use different varieties of apple, and the best cider is made from a single type, such as the *guillevic* apple grown mainly in Morbihan, which produces Royal Guillevic (look for the Label Rouge quality mark). In Morbihan a pear cider called *poiré* is also produced.

For stronger stuff, couchenn is a honey-based spirit, like mead or hydromel, while *lambig* is a fiery apple brandy, good to knock back in one gulp. The aperitif *pommeau* is made from the juice of cider apples and brandy, and sometime used in desserts.

Beer is also produced in Brittany, with growing popularity. You can visit the premises of Coreff, the best known, in Carhaix, for a tour and to buy the product, and also Britt (brasseriedebretagne.com) in southern Finistere, which makes a good range.

When Loire-Atlantique was part of Brittany, it could lay claim also to the robust wine Muscadet, from the Nantes area, which is the traditional accompaniment to shellfish. The white wine Gros Plant is also from the same region.

Festivals in West Coast Brittany

There is always a burst of energy when summer comes and the big festivals draw crowds from far and wide. However, the traditional year-round regular entertainment in Brittany is the fest-noz or fest-deiz (night or day fête) which brings together a local community to eat, dance and sing. Traditional Breton dancing is fascinating to watch, but you will also be welcome to join the circle.

January
Astropolis (date varies), *Brest, astropolis.org*. This popular electro-music festival launched a varied winter version in 2012.

February
Les Hivernautes (third week), *Quimper, hivernautes.com*. With rock, hip-hop and electro-jazz musicians.

April
Fête de la Coquille Saint-Jacques (late

April/early May), *St-Quay Portrieux*. Taking the scallop to new levels with the usual trimmings of song and dance.
Festival les Marionnet'ics, *Binic. ville-binic. fr*. Puppets and marionettes from all over the world performing indoors and out.
Festival de la BD, *Perros-Guirec, bdperros. com*. Celebration of cartoon and comic books (bande-dessinées).

May
Art Rock, *St-Brieuc*, artrock.org. Pulsating music and all manner of street-animations.
Fête de la Morue (third week), *Binic, ville-binic.fr*. Lively celebration of the town's maritime traditions.
Pardon of St-Yves (third Sunday), *Tréguier*. This important pardon for Brittany's patron saint has a huge procession, with lawyers from around the world attending their special patron's festival.

July

Grand/Petit Tromenie (second Sunday), *Locronan*. This pardon has a procession up to the chapel above the town each year. Every six years it takes a much longer form (next in 2013), celebrating an early Christian religious tour said to be based on a sacred Celtic space, with a popular walking event.

Les Vieilles Charrues (third week), *Carhaix-Plouguer, vieillescharrues.asso.fr*. Brittany's answer to Glastonbury. This famous music festival attracts international artists such as Bruce Springsteen and Breton stars, as well as new bands and local talent.

Festival de Cornouaille (second half of July), *Quimper, festival-cornouaille.com*. Quimper devotes itself to a lavish celebration of Breton culture, with pipe bands, concerts, dancing and parades.

August

Festival du Chant de Marin (first weekend), *Paimpol, paimpol.net*. Held every two years (next 2013) this celebrates the maritime tradition of the area with artists from all over the world, on the loose theme of sea shanties.

Festival de Cinéma, *Douarnenez, festival-douarnenez.com*. Outdoor large-screen offerings on a theme with lots of associated festivities.

Festival du Bout du Monde (early August), *Crozon Peninsula, festivalduboutdumonde.com*. Summer music-fest of international appeal, where big stars mix with local talent.

Festival Interceltique (first half) *Lorient, festival-interceltique.com*. The biggest and boldest of the Celtic events, celebrating the diversity and similarity of all the Celtic cultures, featuring Brittany, Scotland, Ireland, Wales, Cornwall, the Isle of Man and Galicia. Each year focuses on one region.

Fête de l'Oignon Rosé (second half of August), *Roscoff, roscoff-tourisme.com*. Around the old port, this popular event pays tribute to the local speciality that sent the Johnnies across the Channel, selling onions to the British from their bicycles.

Les Filets Bleus (second half of August), *Concarneau, filetsbleus.free.fr*. This event recalls attempts made in 1905 to raise support for fishermen, impoverished by the failure of sardine shoals. Now a lively, colourful festival with pageants and music.

Astropolis (date varies), *Brest, astropolis.org*. A four-day feast of electro-music.

Pardon of Ste-Anne (last weekend), *Ste-Anne-la-Palud*.

September

Blessing of the sea (first Sunday), *Camaret, camaret-sur-mer.com*. Pardon and benediction, honouring those lost at sea, with gathering of boats and the local lifeboat.

Pardon de Notre-Dame de Tronoën (third Sunday), *Tronoën, Pays Bigouden*.

October

Fête des Pommes (first half), *St-Rivoal, Monts d'Arrée*. A celebration of the apple harvest with food, music and stalls. Connected festivities around honey and mushrooms take place in nearby Brasparts.

Atlantique Jazz Festival (second half of October), *Finistère, atlantiquejazzfestival.com*. A wide range of music within the genre.

December

Noël à Trévarez, *Château de Trévarez, near Châteauneuf-du-Faou, cdp29.fr*. This château always puts on a good Christmas-themed exhibition and celebration.

Walking in West Coast Brittany

Brittany provides an amazing variety of landscape for all kinds of walking, from challenging to easy strolls. The coastline is exceptional, but the interior also offers a good choice, from verdant river valleys to open moors and wooded countryside.

The GRs are national footpaths organized by the **FFRP** (Fédération Française de la Randonnée Pédestre) that have red and white waymarks, while the **GPR** (red and yellow waymarks) are routes covering places of interest in a particular area. Each *commune* has local, organized circuits, marked in yellow, blue or green and usually shown on a leaflet from the Mairie or tourist office. **IGN** (ign.fr) maps are widely available in supermarkets and bookshops. Their Randonnée editions have major footpaths marked, but these are not always up to date, as things can change quickly on the ground. Long-distance paths or Green Ways, are now in development to provide hundreds of kilometres of fairly level tracks using old railway lines and canal towpaths. An up-to-date summary can be found via **Randobreizh** (randobreizh.com).

Rural footpaths here are usually along communal tracks, the old inter-village routes, not across fields, so there's little problem about rights of way. It's important to take note of diversions marked during the hunting season (September-February), when some paths, especially through privately owned woods, will be closed.

The most spectacular route of all is the coastal path (GR34), former path of the customs officers, running for 2000 km around the Armorican peninsula from Mont St-Michel to just beyond the Gulf of Morbihan. Most of this is close to the shore, hugging the undulating cliffs and coves and providing stunning views of sea, islands and lighthouses. Recommended for a demanding hike are the Crozon Peninsula from Camaret to Morgat, the Cap Sizun peninsula from Douarnenez to Audierne, including the Pointe du Raz, and the cliffs of Plouha on the Côte de Goëlo. If you want the stunning scenery without the constant ups and downs, the Pink Granite coast starting from Perros Guirec is a world-famous marvel and easy walking, or try the Finistère coast west of Roscoff as far as Plougeurneau.

Forest walking is often a good bet for family fun and there are many circuits, both easy and more strenuous, in the area around Huelgoat, with its added bonus of an amazing granite 'chaos' with huge boulders in strange formations around the river Argent.. Other options are the large mixed Forêt du Cranou near Le Faou, the beautiful woods along the Aulne and Rade de Brest at Landévennec or the more regular Forêt de Coatloch near Scaer.,

The Nantes–Brest canal running right across Brittany provides an unproblematic, pretty much level route for strollers or a long-distance option for hardy walkers ready to cover the 365-km length. A two-week holiday will nearly do it! Don't be deceived by the word canal – less than 20% is artificial, the rest is made up of glorious wide-flowing rivers including the mighty Aulne, and the route passes by attractive towns and near chapels and châteaux, as well as some of the loveliest natural scenery imaginable. The Finistere stretch includes pretty Chateauneuf-de-Faou, where boats can be hired, a *centre nautique* at Pont Coblant and the small but bustling town of Chateaulin with its bars and restaurants, where the river flows right through the centre.

For something completely different, the Monts d'Arrée in Finistère is an area of open moors and schist peaks, the highest in Brittany. Circuits there offer stony tracks, wooden walkways across peat bogs and the hilltops of Mont St-Michel de Brasparts with its little chapel or the rounded ridge of Tuchenn Gador. Two exceptional routes of 14km and 18km cover all the best scenery.

If you are based in the Trégor, don't miss the superb 10km circuit starting from the Chateau de Tonquedec, which combines the idyllic banks of the wide Léguer with secular and religious buildings of note, one of the nicest routes in Brittany. The valley of the Trieux estuary also offers good walking and views of the impressive Chateau de la Roche-Jagu.

If you're considering a walking holiday, recommended times would be May, June or September. The paths are never especially busy, but these months usually have the most pleasant weather and temperature for being outside all day. Plan ahead if you're looking for overnight accommodation on a long linear route, as some sections of the coastal path are well off the beaten track and available places can get booked up. It's also important to plan food and water provisions for the same reasons.

This is an incredibly diverse landscape. It's worth remembering that many of Brittany's special delights – lonely menhir, isolated chapels, dazzling promontories, little islands across narrow causeways that vanish at high tide – are only accessible on foot.

Essentials A-Z

Customs and immigration
UK and EU citizens do not need a visa, only a valid passport or identity card. US and Canadian citizens must have a valid national passport. US citizens can check the customs situation through their Customs Service (customs.ustreas.gov).

Disabled travellers
Brittany is gradually providing better access and facilities for disabled visitors. The regional tourist board (tourismebretagne. com) has a download of accommodation adapted for reduced mobility. For wide-ranging information on equipment, activities, including sporting options, transport possibilities and accommodation, have a look at bretagne-accessible.com. This also provides localized details.

Emergencies
Ambulance (SAMU) T15, **Fire service** (Pompiers) T18, **Police** T17. The pan-European emergency number from any phone is T112.

Etiquette
Brittany is still a traditional place with strong social bonds. Good manners are the norm here – it's common to say a general *bonjour* on entering a small shop or the post office, or to people in the street in rural areas. Bretons respond well to a smile and a greeting. Showing respect for religious buildings by speaking quietly and keeping children under control in a cathedral or chapel will also go down well. And do ask before taking a photograph of someone performing their job, whether it's a fisherman or crêpe-maker.

Families
Brittany is just as family friendly as the rest of France. Children are welcomed in restaurants and hotels, and special provision is happily made if necessary. Discounts are usually offered at attractions for children up to 16 years old, and those under four are often given free entrance. Tickets for a *famille nombreuse* give a price for three or more children who are accompanied by two parents.

Health
Comprehensive travel and medical insurance is recommended. EU citizens should apply for a free European Health Insurance Card or EHIC (ehic.org.uk), which entitles you to emergency medical treatment on the same terms as French nationals. Note that you will have to pay all charges and prescriptions up front and be reimbursed once you return home. If you develop a minor ailment while on holiday, a visit to any pharmacy will allow you to discuss your concerns with highly qualified staff, who can give medical advice and recommend treatment. Outside normal opening hours, the address of the nearest duty pharmacy (*pharmacie de garde*) is displayed in the pharmacy window. The out-of-hours number for a local doctor (*médecin généraliste*) may also be listed.

In a serious emergency, go to the accident and emergency department (*urgences*) at the nearest Centre Hospitalier or call an ambulance (SAMU) by dialling T15.

Insurance
Comprehensive travel and medical insurance is strongly recommended, as the European Health Insurance Card (EHIC) does not cover medical repatriation, ongoing medical treatment or treatment considered to be non-urgent. Check for exclusions if you mean to engage in risky sports. Keep all insurance documents to hand; a good way to keep track of your policies is to email the details to yourself. Make sure you have adequate insurance when hiring a

car and always ask how much excess you are liable for if the vehicle is returned with any damage. It is generally worth paying a little more for a collision damage waiver. If driving your own vehicle to France, contact your insurers before you travel to ensure you are adequately covered, and keep the documents in your vehicle in case you need to prove it.

Money
The French currency is the euro. There are plenty of ATMs all over Brittany, in banks, commercial centres, main post offices and often in ferry terminals. Credit and debit cards are not accepted everywhere (look for the signs at restaurants beforehand) so it's a good idea to have cash as well. Small sites and private attractions and even some shops may refuse plastic. Traveller's cheques can be cashed at post offices and banks, in theory, but problems are sometimes experienced and using a cash card will certainly be easier.

Brittany is generally a relatively cheap place for visitors, especially outside the main towns and away from the coast. Even privately owned castles and museums are likely to charge little more than €5 for entry. For refreshments and visits, €50 per person should be enough for a day.

Opening hours
Monday is often closing day for shops, museums and other attractions, and lunchtime closing for most things is usual, except in July and August. Many chapels are closed for most of the year but an enquiry at the nearest house or Mairie will sometimes produce a key. Advertised opening times are usually, but not always, reliable in the main tourist season, but may be changed without notice in the winter months.

Police
The Municipal Police are based in towns and deal with parking, transport issues and civic events. The Gendarmerie deal with traffic and criminal offences and general law and order, while the Police Nationale deal with crime in large towns.

Post
Generally the postal system is reliable and efficient. A letter or postcard to the UK requires a €0.77 stamp, and an €0.89 one for the US and Canada.

Bars usually sell stamps, but these will not be for foreign destinations.

Safety
Brittany is a low-crime area, although common-sense precautions should be taken in cities and at night. Avoid small alleyways and parks after dark. Be sure to lock cars (and bicycles) and don't leave valuables in sight or in the boot. If you are worried about valuables in hotels, ask at reception for safe facilities. Personal safety is unlikely to be an issue.

Telephone
To call France from abroad, dial T00 33 then the number minus the initial 0. The Brittany area code is 02 followed by eight digits. You need to dial the whole number within France. Departmental codes are 96 (Côtes d'Armor), 97 (Morbihan), 98 (Finistère) and 99 (Ille-et-Vilaine). Information calls may begin 08.

Public phone booths take prepaid cards, obtainable from a bar/tabac, newsagents and post offices.

The mobile phone network, split mainly between Orange, SFR and Bouyges Telecom, is reasonable but coverage can be patchy.

Time difference
France uses Central European Time, GMT + 1.

Tipping
Service is almost always included in restaurants and there is no need to leave a tip, although simple rounding up is

appreciated rather than waiting for a few cents of change. This is especially true when taking coffee outside a bar. Tipping in hotels is not expected. For other services such as taxis, tip up to 15%.

Tourist information

The regional committee for tourism has a useful website for all styles of holiday – brittanytourism.com, and bretagne. com is also helpful. Each town has its own website/tourist office.

The *Central Brittany Journal*, an informative English-language monthly magazine available in most newsagents, has a good What's On feature.

Tourist passes

Each department has a passport or similar scheme where linked sites have reduced entry after the first use and at least one free visit if you go to all the relevant places. Some large towns, such as Quimper, have a similar discount offer for main places of interest. Areas with good outdoor facilities may offer a discount scheme for following more than one activity or booking multiple sessions.

Voltage

France functions on a 220v mains supply. Plugs are the standard round two-pin European variety.

Contents

Footprint features

Finistère

Finistère is the most Breton part of Brittany, the starting point for the defence of Breton language and custom, proudly upheld in festivals such as the magnificent Festival de Cornouaille in beautiful Quimper, the departmental capital. Brest, a visually modern city, proclaims its effervescent maritime identity every four years (next time in 2012) in the Fête Maritime Internationale, attracting thousands of boats and hundreds of thousands of visitors. Smaller towns like Morlaix and Douarnenez add further layers of character to the dense history of an area full of contrasting experiences.

The End of the World is fittingly a place of extremes – the highest hills in Brittany, the tallest standing stone in France and the biggest waves, Atlantic breakers storming onto the superlative coastline of the Crozon Peninsula and Pointe du Raz. There's also a stunning landscape in the wild heather-covered moors and peat-bogs of the Monts d'Arrée. It's a place of legend and strong beliefs, a fitting context for one of the finest religious displays in Brittany in the parish closes.

Quimper and Pays Bigouden

Quimper is a wonderful city, administrative capital of Finistère, and home to the famous Festival de Cornouaille each July. Smart modern shops line streets of bright medieval houses around the stunning cathedral and River Odet. To the southwest, Pays Bigouden is a bastion of distinctive customs and traditions, with two museums offering a taster of the very essence of Breton life in Pont l'Abbé and Le Guilvinec, an archetypal fishing port. The extraordinary coastlines around Penmarc'h and St-Guenolé admirably reflect the dangers and pleasures of the coast of Brittany.

Quimper → *For listings, see pages 33-35.*

Quimper is a busy place, historic and highly cultural, but with the successful aura of a small capital city. The word means 'confluence' (*kemper* in Breton), as the Steir and Frout meet the wide Odet here. Unusually the settlement was the domain of the bishop, and ducal authority only began across the Pont Médard near the Place Terre-au-Duc. The cathedral and the bishop's palace, now the Departmental Museum, dominate the ancient heart with its narrow cobbled streets. The oldest house, which dates back to the early 15th century, is to be found in Rue Treuz.

A town tour

Start in the Rue du Parc opposite the impressive Prefecture building on the quay. This was rebuilt after the Germans burnt it on being driven out by the Resistance.

Continue along the river past the *passerelles* (footbridges), a legacy of the south bank being lined by individual grand houses with their own personal bridges. The distinctive wrought-iron modern one is dedicated to Max Jacob; if the water is low you can see his portrait etched on the pillar below. This Quimper artist died in a concentration camp; an ironic twist is that the Ouest-France building across the river, in 'steamboat' style, was the design of Olier Mordrel, architect, Breton nationalist and German collaborator.

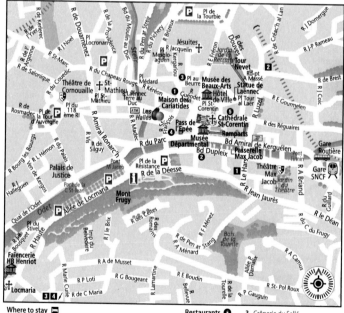

Where to stay 🛏
1 Escale Oceania
2 Hôtel Gradlon
3 Hôtel Oceania
4 Orangerie de Lannion

Restaurants 🍴
1 Bistrot à lire
2 Café des Arts
3 Crêperie du Sallé
4 L'Epée
5 Le Saint Co

Max Jacob

Max Jacob (1876-1944) was a poet, essayist and painter, living in Paris amongst the artists of Montmartre as the Cubist movement developed. He was a friend of Picasso, Modigliani, Cocteau and British painter Kit Wood.

Born a Jew in Quimper, he converted to Catholicism at the age of 40, after seeing visions of Christ. He began to write and paint on religious subjects, and retired to the abbey at St-Benoît-sur-Loire. He was arrested by the Nazis in 1944 and taken to Drancy where he died two weeks later.

Go through the wall doorway by the pretty garden to the cathedral and the **Bishop's Palace**. The latter is mostly 17th century, renewed after fires during the Wars of Religion. The entrance hall of the superb Departmental Museum here is in the original kitchen of 1645, complete with well and bread ovens.

Stand opposite the cathedral's main entrance, at the end of the Rue de Kéréon, to look up at the spires and statue of King Gradlon on horseback; surprisingly both are 19th-century additions. The square here, Place St-Corentin, was the scene of the burning of statues of saints after the revolution.

The **Cathedral of St-Corentin** is famous for its crooked nave, achieved when work restarted after a long break because of the disruption of the Wars of Succession and 14th-century outbreaks of plague. The strange angle may have been because the newly adjoined bishop's palace forced this, or possibly because of problems with earlier foundations or the proximity of the river. More fancifully, some suggest it mirrors the incline of Jesus' head on the cross. An extra half-chapel inside on the south side compensates for the angle.

In the south aisle the bronze tomb of Bishop Du Parc with a frieze of the seven Founding Saints of Brittany has attracted the custom of performing a mini Tro Breizh pilgrimage here, by walking around the tomb, touching seven points of the bishop's effigy. You can see which ones...

On the wall at the east end is the statue and skull of Santig Du, the Little Black Saint, a Franciscan who helped the poor in Quimper and died during the plague of 1349. For 500 years he has been invoked to help find lost items – many today continue this custom, placing loaves of bread on the table below in thanks.

In the north aisle a painting shows Père Maunoir receiving the gift of the Breton tongue from an angel. He came from eastern Brittany and therefore did not speak Breton when he was called to succeed Michel Le Nobletz in missionary work in Basse Bretagne. A miracle or clever 17th-century marketing?

It's worth looking at the Chapel of St-Corentin – the stained-glass window shows an early crêpe pan!

Continue along the Rue de Frout behind the cathedral and then left past the former ramparts. You can see the only tower remaining, the **Tour de Nevet**. Go up the steps just beyond into the **Jardin de la Retraite**, a beautiful refuge being re-modelled at the time of writing, overlooked by the huge Jesuit chapel.

Exit at the other end of the garden and turn left then second right to view old houses in **Place du beurre** and **Rue du Sallé**. A restaurant adorned by caryatid sculptures is in the nearby **Rue du Guéodet**. Turn down to the **indoor market** (Les Halles) in Rue St-François, where you can stock up for lunch with all manner of enticing food, or perhaps have a crêpe made freshly to order. Then continue to the Pont Médard via Rue de Kéréon with its fashionable shops.

Cross the bridge over the Steir, then go left through the square and along **Rue René Madec**. The painted panel at No 5 records this man's extraordinary achievement. Born in Quimper in 1736 of humble origins, he went to sea, and served in India for the Compagnie des Indes. He later entered the private army of the Grand Mogul, and was made a nabob. Continue ahead to return to the Odet and tourist office below **Mount Frugy**, which is a good place for a pause or a climb for views over the city. A cult of the Goddess Reason was set up here at the time of the Revolution.

After lunch, take a peaceful stroll along the Odet to **Locmaria**, the oldest settlement. Pottery was a tradition here even in Roman times and it was revived as a major industry in 1690 by Jean-Baptiste Bousquet. The Musée de la Faïence here records the history and the works of Henriot are still operational today – there is a large shop selling all kinds of pottery with the famous colourful naïf designs. You can also take a tour of the factory to see how the pieces are made. If eating is more appealing, there's a lovely biscuit shop nearby too.

The church of **Notre Dame de Locmaria** is a thrilling example of Romanesque architecture, with remains of the 12th-century cloister through a side door. The **medieval gardens** opposite by the river are a delightful place to take a rest.

Musée Départemental Breton

ⓘ *1 rue du Roi Gradlon, T02 98 95 21 60. Jun-Sep daily 0900-1800, Oct-May 0900-1200, 1400-1700 (closed Mon, Sun morning and public holidays). €4.*

Allow at least an hour to visit the excellent displays here. Modernity blends in with the antiquity of the building, the former Bishop's Palace. The 16th-century turning stair in the Rohan tower has a carved newel post and parasol finish at the top. The exhibition starts on the ground floor with prehistory, Gallo-Romano deities and Roman coin hoards. Religious art of the Middle Ages includes the tombs of knights and statuary, such as the figure of St-Trémeur holding his severed head. Upstairs there are many examples of Breton costumes in all their intricate details and exquisitely carved wooden furniture, together with a display of Quimper pottery. Look out for 1920s ceramics by Pierre Toulhoat, which manage to amalgamate a plethora of Breton motifs in colourful scenes, and an amusing black and white ensemble of peasants and cow by Mathurin Méheut.

Musée des Beaux Arts

ⓘ *40 place St-Corentin, T02 98 95 45 20, mbaq.fr. Open 0930-1200, 1400-1800, closed Tue (except in Jul and Aug), Nov-Mar closed Sun morning. €5.*

Here you'll find a wealth of Breton domestic and outdoor scenes like the Pardon of Kergoat by Jules Breton with its sharp contrasts of celebration and destitute observers. Another room illustrates Breton legends – 'Les Lavandières de la Nuit' (1861) by Yan Dargent shows an unfortunate traveller ensnared by a herd of flying sheets. The most famous tale is St-Guénolé persuading King Gradlon to throw his daughter Dahut into the waves engulfing the city of Ys.

The Salle Max Jacob has a striking portrait by Cocteau, but it's the strange painting showing a sort of martyrdom of Jacob, by Pierre de Belay, that really lingers in the mind. It was painted 10 years before Jacob's death.

Upstairs there are European old masters and the Pont-Aven school's Emile Bernard, Sérusier, Seguin and Maxime Maufra are all represented, plus a goose by Gauguin.

Pays Bigouden → *For listings, see pages 33-35.*

Pont l'Abbé
① *14 km southwest of Quimper.*

This very Breton town is set on an estuary with lovely walks down to Loctudy. It's a place of simple appeal, unspoilt by tourism. Each July the Fêtes des Brodeuses (embroiderers) is celebrated with costumed parades and music filling the streets.

This was the crossing point for the monks at Loctudy – hence the name – and Pont l'Abbé retains the formidable keep of the former château of the Barons du Pont, now an excellent museum. It was partly destroyed in the rebellion of the Bonnets Rouge in 1675, and reprisals for that uprising can be seen in the truncated tower of the church of Lambour, with its fine carvings, just across the water. On the riverside near the Eglise des Carmes, which has a resonant 15th-century rose window, is the moving Bigouden memorial of grieving women by François Bazin.

Musée Bigouden ① *Château des Barons du Pont, T02 98 66 09 03, museebigouden.fr, Apr-May Tue-Sun 1400-1800, Jun-Sep daily 1000-1230, 1400-1830, €3.50.*

The tall lace coiffe has become an image synonymous with Brittany. The name Bigouden comes from this headdress, and its vital story, linked to Breton identity, is told here, partly in the words and experience of individuals. Visiting this museum of social history also allows a look at the keep of the former château, though it's odd to be looking at a 1960s formica kitchen one minute and climbing a medieval turning stone staircase the next. Interesting exhibits look at the changing world of the area, particularly the role of women and the wearing of the famous headdress, at work and play – watching football, for example. There are some beautiful displays of Breton costumes and lacework, the latter becoming an important source of income for families on the breadline after the failure of the sardine catch in the early 20th century.

Le Guilvinec
① *11 km southwest of Pont l'Abbé.*

The essence of life by the sea is epitomized in Le Guilvinec, third fishing port of France. A visit to **Haliotika: La Cité de la Pêche** ① *Le Port, T02 98 58 28 38, haliotika.com, Jul and Aug Mon-Fri 0930-1900, Sat and Sun 1500-1830, Mar-Jun and Sep 1000-1230, 1430-1830, Oct Mon-Fri 1500-1800, €5.90/€3.90,* gives an insight into the marine world of work with displays on different types of boats, fish of all kinds and a recreation of workers' life at sea. Much is relayed through the life and words of one former fisherman Claude Garo, which gives a personal perspective. There are also colourful exhibits for children and a chance to sit in the captain's hot-seat.

Penmarc'h
① *12 km southwest of Pont l'Abbé.*

This southwestern tip of Brittany, Penmarc'h ('horse's head' in Breton) was once a major European trading centre, at the turning-point between north and south. The ship motifs decorating the large church here reflect the prosperity brought by the sea in medieval times. Today you can appreciate the extreme difficulties of navigation around this area by climbing the 272 steps of the lighthouse. The magnificent **Phare Eckmuhl** ① *Apr-Sep 1030-1830,* was constructed from Kersanton granite in the 1890s after the daughter of one of Napoleon's generals left a legacy for a lighthouse in a dangerous environment to honour her father's memory.

St-Guénolé

ⓘ *15 km southwest of Pont l'Abbé.*

Chaucer's Franklin's Tale begins with reference to the fearful *blakes rokkes* of Penmarc'h, the rocks that Dorigen fears will cost the life of her husband on return from England, so she hires a magician to make them disappear. Follow signs to **Les Rochers**, and climb carefully up to the railing. The iron cross on the rock ahead marks the spot where family members of the Prefect of Finistère were swept away to their deaths when picnicking in 1870.

A safer spot is **Porz Carn**, one of the nicest family beaches imaginable. Opposite the car park is the **Musée de la Préhistoire** ⓘ *T02 98 58 60 35, Jun-Sep Mon-Fri 1030-1230, 1400-1800, Sun 1430-1730, closed Sat, otherwise afternoons only in school holidays*, with many indoor and outdoor exhibits from archaeological digs in Finistère. There's a rare Dark Age offering, with the remains of some of the first Bretons from the nearby burial ground (c AD 50-1000) of St-Urnel.

Pointe de la Torche

ⓘ *12 km southwest of Pont l'Abbé.*

On the headland itself is a large Neolithic dolmen, in striking contrast with the German fortifications around it. The magnificent beach, exposed to the driving wind and waves of the Atlantic, is a well known surfing mecca, and many come just to watch the performers. If you want to join in, the **Ecole de Surf de Bretagne** ⓘ *T02 98 58 53 80*, has a base here.

You can walk for many miles up the beach, past bunkers and, at Croaz an Dour (3 km), remains of the factory where the Germans ground pebbles into concrete for all their defensive works, at great cost to the natural protective pebble banks of this exposed coast.

Tronoën

ⓘ *11 km southwest of Pont l'Abbé.*

The chapel here is often called the Cathedral of the Dunes, as its spire is visible for miles. The calvary is possibly the oldest in Brittany (c 1450). In granite, with statues in darker Kersanton, parts are eroded, but you can clearly make out scenes such as Ste-Veronica and the face of Christ imprinted on her handkerchief, and the three kings bringing gifts. In fact, there are 30 scenes, perhaps the most remarkable being that of Mary with naked breasts and tousled hair on the lower frieze.

Quimper and Pays Bigouden listings

For Sleeping and Eating price codes and other relevant information, see page 13.

🛏 Where to stay

Quimper *p28, map p28*
€€€-€€ Hôtel Gradlon, *30 rue de Brest, Quimper, T02 98 95 04 39, hotel-gradlon.com.* Best choice for central Quimper, with quiet off-street rooms available around a pretty interior courtyard garden complete with fountain. Rooms are tastefully decorated and well equipped. There's no restaurant, but guests can enjoy a comfy bar and an excellent buffet breakfast Is served in or overlooking the garden. Impeccable service. Parking available (paid).

€€€-€€ Hôtel Oceania, *17 rue du Poher, Quimper, T02 98 90 46 26, oceaniahotels. com.* This modern hotel has spacious rooms with sleek modern decor, air conditioning and comfortable beds. Facilities include an outdoor heated swimming pool (summer months only), free parking and Wi-Fi. Catering is not that special – the restaurant kitchen can be very slow even when it's not especially busy, and you can get much better value for money breakfasts at the nearby commercial centre.

€€ Escale Oceania, *6 rue Théodore Le Hars, Quimper, T02 98 53 37 37, oceaniahotels.com.* A cheaper Oceania hotel, newly refurbished for 2012. in an excellent position for the cathedral and centre, just across one of the river passerelles. Rooms are decent, and there's a restaurant, although you're well placed for access to many others. A useful multi-storey car park is right next door.

Self-catering/camping
Orangerie de Lanniron, *Allée de Lanniron, T02 98 90 62 02, lanniron.com.* The most beautiful setting in the grounds of a (private) château for this 'one-stop shop' for accommodation, with camping, chalets to rent and even overnight hotel facilities. On the banks of the Odet, there's also a large outdoor swimming pool, and bikes for hire. The little boathouse for two is ideal for a romantic holiday. Camping is €20-41 per night, chalet rental €450-1000 a week.

Pays Bigouden *p31*
€€€-€€ Hôtel/Restaurant Le Poisson d'Avril, *19-21 rue Men Meur, Le Guilvinec, T02 98 58 23 83, lepoissondavril.fr.* Well-positioned hotel near the port and Haliotika discovery centre. The bedrooms are in rustic/marine chic style with colourful fabrics and good bathrooms. A suite of two rooms is available for a family. Try to get a room with a private terrace and fantastic sea views. If you can't get one of these, the outdoor dining area offers the same thing.

🍴 Restaurants

Quimper *p28, map p28*
€€ L'Epée, *14 rue du Parc, T02 98 95 28 97, quimper-lepee.com.* Daily 1030-2300 (food served 1200-1430, 1900-2200). A suave brasserie by the river with flavoursome food and cheerful service. Modern decor and music set the scene for varied menus, with a three-course lunch just over €20. A puff pastry artichoke tart might be followed by crisp-skinned cod and imaginatively cooked vegetables. The chocolate pannacotta is a richly satisfying dessert. Good ambience, popular with all ages.

€€ Le Saint Co, *20 rue du Frout, T02 98 95 11 47. le-saint-co.com.* Lunch and dinner all year Mon-Sat, closed Feb. This restaurant behind the cathedral has set menus at €20.50 and €26.50 offering oysters, scallops and salmon as well as steak with a choice of sauces. Tender pork fillet in mustard sauce comes with chunky potato wedges and a selection of vegetables. Cheaper lunch options available. Don't be deterred by the poky interior, as there is also an upstairs room.

€ Crêperie du Sallé, *6 rue du Sallé, T02 98 95 95 80. 1200-1400, 1900-2230, closed Sun and Mon*. In the heart of the old town, with tables on the street or a dining room with ancient beams and Breton-themed decorative plates. The menu is fairly basic, but crêpes are tasty with quality fillings. Particular recommendations include pear and hot chocolate, and apples with salted caramel. At busy times of year queues form at lunchtime, so get there early, although service is pretty brisk.

Cafés and bars
€ Bistrot à lire, *18 rue des Boucheries, T02 98 95 30 86. Mon 1400-1900, Tue-Sat 0900-1900*. A bookshop with café. Simple lunches and cakes available.

€ Café des Arts, *4 rue Ste-Catherine, T02 98 90 32 06. Mon-Fri 1100-0100, Sat and Sun 1500-0100*. On the quieter bank of the river, with a cathedral view from the outdoor tables, this café/bar is popular with arty types and young people. Linger over hot drinks, beer and cocktails (including non-alcoholic). You can even try Guinness with a squirt of caramel syrup.

Pays Bigouden *p31*
€€-€ Auberge du Port, *74 rue de la Marine, Le Guilvinec, T02 98 58 14 60. Open mid-Mar to mid-Sep, lunch and dinner every day*. Slightly old-fashioned feel for this family-run restaurant, with dark blue paint and tablecloths, but the food is excellent, particularly a huge plate of fruits de mer (shellfish) fresh from the port. A simple meal of flavoursome fish soup, white fish fillet of the day in tangy seaweed sauce and home-made crème caramel costs all of €16!

€ Crêperie Les 4 Saisons, *2 rue Burdeau, Pont l'Abbé, T02 98 87 06 05. Daily 1130-1400, 1830-2100, except mid-Sep to Apr closed Sun*. An unpretentious place just off the main street with memorable offerings, from the savoury blé noir with goat's cheese, streaky bacon and a sort of creamy prune sauce to the Bigouden speciality dessert crêpe 'au riz

au lait', a sweet rice pudding filling flavoured with caramel or chocolate or apple.

🎭 Entertainment

Quimper *p28, map p28*
Festivals and events
Festival de Cornouaille, *festival-cornouaille. com*. This iconic annual festival (programme and tickets from March) in July fills the historic centre with music, song and dance. A chance to learn Breton dancing, listen to traditional instruments and watch children parade in colourful costumes. Many events are free.

Music
Le Ceili, *4 rue Aristide Briand, T02 98 95 17 61. Mon-Sat 1030-0100, Sun 1700-0100*. The best place for traditional music in a lively ambience. Also worth a visit for the choice of more than 20 beers, including the pick of local brews.
Théâtre de Cornouaille, *1 esplanade François Mitterand, T02 98 55 98 55, theatre-cornouaille.fr. Season runs Sep-Jun, closed Sun*. Concerts, theatre and spectacles all year round. Many modern and innovative productions, with world music well represented. You can book online.

Pays Bigouden *p31*
Festivals and events
Fêtes des Brodeuses, *fetedesbrodeuses.com*. This festival of embroiderers is celebrated in Pont l'Abbé in July with costumed parades and lively music filling the streets.

🛍 Shopping

Quimper *p28, map p28*
Arts and crafts
Henri Faïence, *Locmaria, Quimper, T02 98 90 09 36, hb-henriot.com. Open 1000-1900, closed 1300-1400 out of season*. This is an outlet for the famous Quimper pottery, in new ownership at the time of writing, so changes of design expected. Factory tours are also possible.

Musée de la Faïence de Quimper, *14,
rue Jean-Baptiste Bousquet, Locmaria, T02
98 90 12 72, musee-faience-quimper.com,
Jun-Sep 1000-1800, closed public holidays.*
This exquisite pottery collection has recently
re-opened to the public.

Food
Les Halles, *Rue St-François*. The indoor
market has all manner of good things –
sushi, Moroccan specialities, local meats and
cheeses, organic bread, fruit and vegetables.
Also many takeaway options for salads,
sandwiches and savouries. Crêpes are freshly
made in front of you, but go before or after
the 1200 rush.
Les Macarons de Philomène, *13 rue Kéréon,
T02 98 95 21 40, macaron-quimper.com. Open
0900-1900, closed Sun and Mon*. This shop
is something of an institution and queues
in the street are not unknown. Macaroons
taken to an art form, in every colour
imaginable.

Pays Bigouden *p31*
Océane Alimentaire, *Le Port, St-Guénolé, T02
98 58 43 04, oceane-alimentaire.com*. Daily in
summer, varied hours in winter. Lots of fish
products, such as rillettes of mackerel and
tuna, seaweed items to eat or to indulge the
body in the form of creams and gels. Free
exhibition.

Transport

Quimper *p28, map p28*
Parking in Quimper is easiest on the quay
past the tourist office or follow signs to
Parking Théodore Le Hars for a convenient
multi-storey; the centre is small enough to
walk around.

Bus
For the local bus network, T02 98 95 26 27,
qub.fr.

Train
Place Louis Armand. TGV links to Brest (1¼
hours) and Paris (about 5 hours).

Directory

Quimper *p28, map p28*
Banks Crédit Agricole, 10 rue René Madec.
Hospital Avenue Yves Thépot, T02 98 52
60 60. **Pharmacy** 24 Place St-Corentin.
Post office Boulevard Amiral de Kerguelen.
Tourist information Place de la Résistance,
T02 98 53 04 05, quimper-tourisme.com,
July and August 0900-1900, otherwise
0930-1230, 1330-1830. **Finistère region:**
finisteretourisme.com.

Brest and around

Brest is a lively maritime city, with several ports, many major nautical events and a formidable history. Another draw is Océanopolis, one of the most visited attractions in France. The Rade de Brest is the largest roadstead in Europe, a veritable inland sea protected by a narrow channel from the might of the Atlantic Ocean. The pretty port of Le Conquet thrives on fish and ferries to Molène and Ouessant, which has a lighthouse museum. Inland, near the interesting town of St-Renan, is the king of all menhirs.

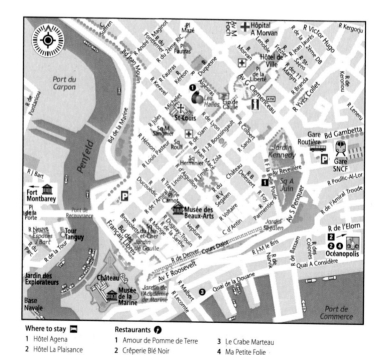

Where to stay 🛏	Restaurants 🍴	
1 Hôtel Agena	1 Amour de Pomme de Terre	3 Le Crabe Marteau
2 Hôtel La Plaisance	2 Crêperie Blé Noir	4 Ma Petite Folie

Brest → *For listings, see pages 40-43.*

On first sight Brest is not particularly attractive. A new tramway is being built (scheduled to open in June 2012), after the last one closed some 40 years ago, and the main square, Place de la Liberté, is a wasteland of concrete, surrounded by fast-food outlets. However, there is a lot more to the city and its many attractions than the superficial impression of modern regularity. And it's important to bear in mind the positive symbolism of the city's resurrection from the ashes.

Brest is essentially a post-war place, thrown up in a hurry to re-house the population after devastating bombing in the Second World War when the German submarine base was a prime allied target. Since the 17th century it has been the main French naval base on the Atlantic coast. Allow at least a day for the city itself and another day for visiting Océanopolis.

Rue de Siam

This is the main street and principal shopping area, leading up from the Pont de Recouvrance over the river to the Place de la Liberté, where you can find the tourist office. The name comes from the exotic visit of ambassadors from the King of Siam in 1686, on their way to Paris and the court of Louis XIV.

Cours Dajot

This long promenade above the commercial port and new docks 'Port du Château' is the best place for a stroll, with fantastic views over the Rade. It was built in 1769 by convicts from the naval prison and later extended to nearly 600 m, starting near the château. The tall monument is to American naval losses in the First World War, rebuilt in identical style after being destroyed by the Germans in 1941. After dark, the Cours is a popular gay meeting place.

Eglise St-Louis

The first stone of this extraordinary structure was laid in 1955, after an earlier church was destroyed in 1944 by the Germans. It is a huge luminous space, with an incredible capacity of 2500 people, and at 85x27 m, the largest post-war church in France. Most expressive is the vast Wall of Lamentation, a contrast to the light pouring in symbolically from the east through stunning plain-glass windows by Maurice Rocher, with stylized figures – Old Testament greats and four Breton saints – like a design for chess-pieces. Behind a row of towering concrete pillars, the wooden confessionals lining the side-aisle look more like changing rooms or saunas. By the entrance is the decorative blue glass baptistery with its modernist font.

Château de Brest/Musée de la Marine

ⓘ *Rue du Château, T02 98 22 12 39, musee-marine.fr. Daily Apr-Sep 1000-1830, Oct-Dec and Feb-Mar 1330-1830 (closed Jan). €5.50*
Reopening after extensive works in April 2012, the former château, which remarkably survived the war almost unscathed, is now home of the Atlantic naval command and the National Marine Museum. A Roman *castellum* has left distinctive stonework separated by layers of tiles visible on the way to the entrance. The castle was held by the English for 50 years in the 14th century during the Wars of Succession, and developed later by Vauban, Louis XIV's military architect, for Atlantic coast defence. The well laid out museum has important nautical exhibits, but the outdoor space is especially interesting with its

perspective of the Rade and Penfeld estuary, where the arsenal and construction yards once stood. The Tour Azenor adds a romantic touch, with the legend of a young pregnant wife imprisoned by the jealousy of her stepmother.

Museé des Beaux Arts

ⓘ *24 rue Traverse, T02 98 00 87 96. Tue-Sat 1000-1200, 1400-1800, Sun 1400-1800, closed Mon. €4.*

This gallery has an interesting variety of Breton scenes on the ground floor, including many examples of the Pont-Aven school. Upstairs are European paintings from the 17th to 19th centuries, and the basement houses temporary exhibitions. The lower rooms are dominated by those essential themes of Breton-inspired art – the sea and women. Bernard and Maufra are well-represented, as are Sérusier, Lacombe and Séguin – look out for the soft and pensive features of the latter's pastel study *La Bretonne*. A study for the ceiling of the theatre in Rennes by Lemordant shows a chain of Breton dancers strutting their stuff up in the clouds. Offerings from Paul Sérusier include a pair of paintings, with women carrying water and laundry bags. A 20th-century perspective is that of the inimitable Mathurin Méheut with his huge brown and grey study of fish (1931).

La Tour Tanguy

ⓘ *Recouvrance. Jun-Sep daily 1000-1200, 1400-1900, Oct-May Wed and Thu 1400-1700, Sat and Sun 1400-1800. Free.*

This restored 14th-century round tower on the banks of the Penfeld is now a museum devoted to the history of Brest. The many fascinating exhibits are engagingly visual, such as huge diaporamas including one of the famous battle scene of the Cordelière, a ship built for Anne de Bretagne and blown up by its own commander in a notorious fight with the English at the mouth of the Rade in 1512. A series of photographs of pre-war Brest strike home the incredible transformation of the city, and paintings show the amazing bustle of the port and arsenal in its heyday. It's strange to see pictures of the old tramway – abolished only in 1970 in the interests of modern development and now reinstated.

Nearby is the **Jardin des Explorateurs**, with a high walkway giving excellent views over the Rade.

Around Brest → *For listings, see pages 40-43.*

Moulin Blanc

ⓘ *3 km east of Brest.*

This is the pleasure port, the largest on the Atlantic coast. Many major and minor sailing events are held here, and there's a constant buzz of aquatic activity, with lots to watch from the bars and promenade, even for non-sailors. Trips with Azenor start here (see What to do, page 43), and behind the port are the white pavilions of Océanopolis.

Océanopolis

ⓘ *Port de Plaisance, Moulin Blanc, T02 98 34 40 40, oceanopolis.com. May to mid-Sep daily 0900-1800 (0900-1900 in Jul and Aug), Oct-Apr 1000-1700, closed Mon except in school holidays. €17.05/11.85.*

This marine life centre is hard to beat for entertainment and education. Apart from the living exhibits, there is an emphasis on the explanatory and informative, with many films and interactive features. Adults and children cannot fail to be entranced not only by perennial favourites, such as penguins and seals, but also the mesmeric tropical shark tanks and luminous jellyfish. Mammals, fish and oceanic plants of every imaginable shape, size and colour are on display. The huge site is divided into Temperate (with an emphasis on Brittany), Tropical and Polar exhibitions. Buy tickets online in advance to save money and avoid the queues.

Conservatoire Botanique National and the Valley of Stang-Alar
ⓘ *3 km east of Brest.*
Almost a hidden valley on the edge of the city near Océanopolis, this is a great place to avoid crowds in verdant surroundings. A pretty stream connects a series of lakes over 2 km, with many paths and picnic areas, as well as a good crêperie (see Restaurants, page 41) and playground. The work of the Conservatoire Botanique National is to preserve endangered species of plants, through conservation and propagation, including threatened native species of the Armorican peninsula. The exhibition room is free, but you pay to visit the greenhouses ⓘ *Apr-Jun, Sep-Oct 0900-1900, Jul to Aug 0900-2000*, with their different temperature and soil-type zones, a must for serious plant lovers.

St-Renan
ⓘ *10 km northwest of Brest.*
Founded by the Irish monk Ronan, this town rose to be capital of the area until losing this status to Brest in 1681. It has always been a busy commercial centre, famous for its markets, today held on Saturdays. The Vieux-Marché is surrounded by medieval merchants' houses, the best of all (1641) now housing a crêperie (see Restaurants, page 41). At the beginning of the 19th century, there were 78 inns for 179 houses here!

The **Maison du Patrimoine** ⓘ *all year Sat 1030-1200, plus Jul and Aug Tue-Sat 1500-1800*, is a little museum of local history in Rue St-Mathieu. There is also a historical trail to follow around the town – a leaflet is available from the tourist office. In the mid-20th century, the excavation of pewter ore became a major, but short-lived, source of prosperity here. The series of lakes around the town are a reminder of this industry, and they now provide good leisure facilities. Lac de Ty Colo has a walking circuit, and fishing and sailing are possible.

Menhir de Kerloas Some 4 km west of St-Renan is the tallest standing stone in France. The Menhir de Kerloas, dating to c 3000 BC, is nearly 11 m high and has the nickname The Hunchback because of two protrusions. Newly-weds would rub against these as part of a fertility ritual, in the hope of having sons. The stone on its rise is visible from 30 km away and may have been sited to be seen from the sea, possibly part of a chain with the many other menhirs in this area.

Fort du Dellec
ⓘ *8 km west of Brest.*
The Goulet or entry channel to the Rade de Brest is lined by fortifications ranging from Vauban forts to German bunkers. The coastal path passes Fort du Dellec, which is now a public park, open every day. The gun-batteries have become viewing platforms with superb views over the water and across to the Pointe des Espagnols. Despite its history, this is a lovely tranquil spot for picnics or playing games. In term time it is very popular with students from the nearby Technopole.

Le Conquet

ⓘ *22 km west of Brest.*

This most picturesque of fishing ports is still a working harbour, and ferries to the islands of Molène and Ouessant leave from here daily. You can watch this spectacle from the Place St- Christophe, where women used to wait anxiously for the return of the fishermen's ships.

The majority of houses in the village were destroyed in an English attack in 1558, but the fine Maison des Seigneurs (1510) in Rue Troadec (its three stair turrets are visible from across the estuary) survived the onslaught. By contrast, the modern hotel on the hill above the port must be one of the ugliest and most inappropriate buildings in Brittany.

The main church contains the tomb of Michel de Nobletz, the influential 17th-century missionary in Brittany who invented painted 'maps' on sheepskin to tell biblical stories to illiterate peasants. The little chapel of Dom Michel above the port in Le Conquet has some representations of these taolennou.

Pointe St-Mathieu

There's a dramatic clifftop setting here for the skeletal remains of the ruined Benedictine Abbaye St-Mathieu. According to legend, Breton sailors brought the original relic, the skull of the Apostle St Matthew, back from Africa. The impressive fire-tower, which the monks operated as an early form of lighthouse, can still be seen, but is now dwarfed by the 19th-century version. Just below the abbey is a First World War memorial by sculptor René Quilivic. From the coastal path here are some fine views of the islands of Quéménez, Molène and Ouessant, and dolphins are a common sight.

Brest and around listings

For Sleeping and Eating price codes and other relevant information, see page 13.

🛏 Where to stay

Brest *p37*

€€ Hôtel La Plaisance, *37/41 rue du Moulin Blanc, T02 98 42 33 33, hotelplaisance.fr.*
Overlooking the pleasure port at Moulin Blanc, this is a perfect base for Océanopolis (200 m) or for taking a boat trip around the Rade. The hotel is modern and plain, but the comfortable rooms are a decent size, many with sea views, some with little balconies. Friendly staff work around the clock, if you want a drink or cup of tea in the middle of the night.

€€-€ Hôtel Agena, *10 rue Frégate la Belle Poule, T02 98 33 96 00, agena-hotel.com.*
If you want a reasonably priced, basic stopping place near the lively commercial port area, this is a good choice. No frills, but acceptable rooms with nautical motifs and a bar area. It's fairly easy to park in the vicinity, and handy for the Cours Dajot. It's only a short walk to the ferries to catch the early boat to Molène or Ouessant.

Around Brest *p38*

€€€ Ferme Insulaire de Quéménès, *T06 63 02 15 08, iledequemenes.fr.* This small island in the Mer d'Iroise is the object of a durable development project. The sole inhabitants, David and Soizic, run a farm, and offer *chambres d'hôtes* with full board. There are only three rooms, with one bathroom between them. Visitors are collected by boat (weather permitting) from the island of Molène. Minimum stay is two nights, which will cost €350-465 all in for two. You will need to book a long time in advance.

€€€-€€ Hostellerie de la Pointe St-Mathieu, *Pointe St-Mathieu, T02 98 89 00 19, pointe-saint-mathieu.com.* It is a real treat to stay in this hotel near the fabulous Pointe St-Mathieu. Rooms have sea views, some overlooking the lighthouse and ruined abbey on the clifftop. Decor is mostly marine

Self-catering
Le Village Vacances de Beauséjour, *Le Conquet, T02 98 89 09 21, lesvillagesmer.com.* Open all year. Well placed for a stroll into town or to the coastal path, this park has good-quality units to rent and is popular with walkers and cyclists. Chalets for 10 (five bedrooms) or for four to five (two bedrooms), both types with kitchen/sitting areas and small outdoor space. Excellent value at €290-600 a week for the smaller model. Short breaks also possible.

🅡 Restaurants

Brest *p37*
€€ Le Crabe Marteau, *8 quai de la Douane, T02 98 33 38 57, crabemarteau.fr. Mon-Sat, lunch and dinner.* In the commercial port where there are many restaurants, this is really one for the seafood lover – the crab and hammer sounds like a gimmick, but the quality and quantity of fresh crab, served with bread, local organic potatoes and sauces on a wooden board is quite an experience. The hammer is more of a wooden mallet! Other fish and shellfish dishes available if you can't face the hard work.

€€ Ma Petite Folie, *Rue Notre Dame du Bon Port, T02 98 42 44 42, ma-petitefolie.com. 1200-1400, 1930-2200, closed Sun.* Due to reopen in 2012 after storm damage, this is a fun place to eat, on board an old boat. The main dining room is the lower deck, with timbers and portholes. If you prefer the upper deck with views over the port, book specifically in advance. The menu is predominantly fishy, with a daily special, but the pork with stir-fried vegetables and the gingered lamb are supremely tender. Set menus have very limited choice for the main course, but there's plenty on offer à la carte.

themed, both smart and comfortable, with a jolly bar in ocean-liner style. The antiquity of the building is apparent in the restaurant with its exposed stone walls and fireplace.

€€-€ Amour de Pomme de Terre, *23 rue des Halles St-Louis, T02 98 43 48 51. 1200-1430, 1900-2200.* A good central place to eat, with huge platters of food figuring the eponymous potato in some form or other. The atmosphere is cheery, with an open kitchen, and chunky rustic tables packed into the small room. There's also a rather basic outdoor terrace opposite. Daily specials may be meat or fish, and the salads are also substantial. Try and find room for the banana tarte tatin if it's on the dessert board. This is not a place for dieters!

€ Crêperie Blé Noir, *Vallon du Stang-Alar, T02 98 41 84 66. Daily 1200-2130.* The restaurant is near the parking area for the Stang Alar valley, with a lake and playground nearby. Crêpes, salads and a few gratin dishes, such as scallops à la Bretonne available. Tasty choice of pancakes like La Bretonne, which has artichokes with ham and cheese. It's a very pleasant place to eat or have a drink outside, not far from Océanopolis.

Around Brest
€ Crêperie La Maison d'Autrefois, *7 rue de l'Eglise, St-Renan, T02 98 32 67 91. 1145-1400, 1900-2130, Sep-Jun closed Wed.* You can enjoy this remarkable 15th-century house, really good crêpes and more at the same time. Sit out in the square and admire the unusual 'helmet' roofline, or in the beamed dining room with turning stair. The speciality Dolmen has sausage from Molène, fried apples, salicorne and a glass of Chouchen spirit. Friendly service, recommended.

€ L'Armen, *9 rue Lieutenant Jourden, Le Conquet, T02 98 89 07 03. Open 1200-1500, 1830-2200, Sep-Jun closed Tue.* A pizzeria that also serves a range of traditional dishes in set menus, such as fish terrine followed by turkey escalope in cream sauce. Friendly and good-humoured service creates a pleasant ambience here, as pizza deliveries stream in and out. Might be worth trying a takeaway to eat by the estuary.

€ Les Korrigans, *7 rue Lieutenant Jourden, Le Conquet, T02 98 89 00 45. Open 1200-1400, 1900-2130*. This crêperie is in a lovely old building, and great if you don't get the grumpy service sometimes on offer. Food is good enough though, with excellent crêpes, especially those stuffed with seafood, as you'd expect in a fishing port.

😄 Entertainment

Bars and clubs
If you're looking for lively bars, music and impromptu performances In Brest, take an evening stroll around the streets by the Port de Commerce.

Brest also has a lively gay scene. The **Pink Sauna** (35 rue Duperré, T02 98 80 68 57, daily from 1200 – from 1300 Sat and Sun – until late) is a popular meeting place with its bar, jacuzzi and sauna rooms and generous opening hours. Of the bars, the pick is **L'Happy Café** (193 rue Jean Jaurés, T02 98 33 62 93, Tue-Sat 1700-0100), a gay bar with dancing and theme nights.

Festivals and events
Fête Maritime Internationale. *Every 4 years in Jul, lestonnerresdebrest2012.fr*. Happening in July 2012, this magnificent festival attracts thousands of boats from all around the world and hundreds of thousands of visitors to Brest for regattas, parades and lavish firework displays over the Rade.

Music
Espace Vauban, *17 av Clémenceau, T02 98 46 06 88, cabaretvauban.com*. A basement cabaret venue with a mainly young crowd. Saturday night is for dancing with a DJ mixing old favourites and current smashes. There's a good jazz programme too.
La Carenne, *30 rue Jean-Marie Le Bris, T02 98 46 06 00, lacarenne.fr*. Home of contemporary music in Brest, with performance space and recording studios. Good place to hear new bands and innovative sounds.
Le Quartz Theatre, *Place de la Liberté, T02 98 33 70 70, lequartz.com. Tue-Sat 1300-1900, later on performance nights, closed Jul and Aug*. The traditional arts centre near the tourist office, with a programme of plays, concerts and dance.
Les Jeudis du Port. In July and August, every Thursday evening is music night in the commercial port area with several stages and lots of street entertainment. International artists feature and recent star-turns include the Yardbirds.

🛍 Shopping

The tourist office has a leaflet – *Brest Shopping* – which lists by category the main shops (especially clothing) in the city centre and a few restaurants. The covered market, Halles St-Louis, with many food stalls, is open daily except Sunday afternoon.

Books
Dialogues, *Forum Roull/rue de Siam, T02 98 44 88 68. Mon-Sat 0930-1930, closed Sun*. The best and largest bookshop in northern Finistère.

Souvenirs
Roi de Bretagne, *12 quai de la Douane, T02 98 46 09 00, roidebretagne.com. Mon-Sat 0930-1900*. Regional products from food to crafts and beauty products.

🏰 What to do

National Marine Naval Base, *Porte de la Grande Rivière, La Corniche, T02 98 22 06 12*. Free visits without reservation to the marine base from mid-June to mid-September (arrive between 1400 and 1500), but you must have a passport or identity card for a country in the European Union. Guided in groups, the visit lasts two hours, often with the chance to go on board a warship.

Boat trips
Azenor, *Port de Plaisance (also Port de Commerce)*, *T02 98 41 46 23, azenor.fr*. This company has daily cruises on the Rade in high season, lasting 1½ hours at a cost of €15.50 (€11.50). There is also a longer option going around the Bay of Camaret, and lunch/dinner events.

Penn ar Bed, *Port de Commerce, Brest, or Ste-Evette, Audierne, T02 98 80 80 80, pennarbed. fr*. Boats go to Molène and Ouessant from Brest (or Le Conquet) all year round. About 30 return June to September, or €19 October to May. Leaving from Brest gives a wonderful trip around Pointe St-Mathieu. For the little island of Sein, boats go from Audierne.

⊖ Transport

It's easy to get around the grid-plan streets in the centre of Brest on foot. Easiest parking (free) is down by the commercial port (five minutes' walk up to the château), or there are underground car parks near the Halles St-Louis and Place de la Liberté.

Bus
The bus station (T08 10 81 00 29) is in Place du 19ème RI. Bus information from Bibus Accueil, 33 avenue G Clemenceau, bibus.fr.

You can get a bus (line 15) to Océanopolis, which is 3 km from the centre. Buses also run to Le Conquet (line 31) and St-Renan (line 32). Ticket €1.30 or 10 for €10.90, one day ticket €3.50.

Tram
The new tramway opens in 2012 (letrambrest.fr). 27 stations will connect residential areas with the centre, where the stops Liberté, Siam and Chateau may cut down a bit of walking time, or use Recouvrance to visit the Tour Tanguy on the Penfeld river. Expected price is €1.35 per journey.

Train
The train station (T36 35, sncf.fr) is next to the bus station in Place du 19ème RI.

ⓘ Directory

Banks ATMs at main Post Office, 13 avenue Georges Clemenceau, 24 hour at Moulin Blanc. **Medical services** Hospital: Hôpital Morvan, 2 avenue Foch, T02 98 22 33 33. **Pharmacy** 36 rue de Siam or 2 place de la Liberté. Post office 90 rue de Siam or Place Général Leclerc. **Tourist information** Office de Tourisme, Place de la Liberté, T02 98 44 24 96, brest-metropolis-tourisme.fr.

The Crozon Peninsula

Called the Presqu'île de Crozon (almost an island), this long peninsula has many aspects, with the northern coast largely occupied by military installations. The Atlantic seaboard has towering cliffs interspersed by superb beaches, with the GR34 coastal path providing unforgettable views in return for a little exercise. The more energetic will find all manner of water sports readily available in Morgat or Camaret, both delightful ports.

Be aware that in August traffic flows into the resorts as continually as waves lap the shore. Access is either via Le Faou, a scenic route crossing the suspension bridge over the Aulne, or via Châteaulin below the lofty height of Menez Hom.

Landévennec → *For listings, see pages 47-49.*

ⓘ *Via D60, 7 km off the main road D791 (on to peninsula from Le Faou).*
This tranquil waterside village, empty out of season, enjoys something of a microclimate, with palm trees and exotic flowers. There's a huge 20th-century abbey (the large shop sells sweets made by the monks) on the hill, but down by the shore are the impressive remains of an earlier abbey, put into context by an excellent modern museum – **Musée de l'Ancienne Abbaye de Landévennec** ⓘ *T02 98 27 35 90, musee-abbaye-landevennec. fr, Apr-May Sun-Fri 1030-1800, Jul-Sep daily 1000-1900, Oct-Mar Sun school holidays only, €5.* This vividly presents the life of the Benedictine monks, including a recreated scriptorium with utensils and dyes used to produce the fine illustrated manuscripts. St-Guénolé, one of the most influential Breton saints, first settled here, but the site was later sacked by marauding Vikings in AD 913, as archaeological evidence shows. It's a beautiful spot, with herb gardens and apple orchards.

Crozon → *For listings, see pages 47-49.*

ⓘ *Via D887, both roads into peninsula lead to Crozon.*
The hub of the holiday area, Crozon is the place to stock up with provisions – there's plenty of choice at the Wednesday market or shops, including a fishmonger, in the pretty centre around the church. The church has an extraordinary altarpiece of the 10,000 martyrs, which has the style of a comic strip, although the story it tells is the tragic one of a whole troop of soldiers put to death for their Christian faith by the Roman emperor Hadrian. The main tourist office for the area is in the former station on the ring road.

Camaret → *For listings, see pages 47-49.*

ⓘ *8 km northwest of Crozon.*
The first submarine tests were held in Camaret in 1801 after Napoleon commissioned the American Robert Fulton to develop his idea, but the town's traditional claim to fame has been as a major lobster-fishing centre, and there are plenty of restaurants to sample the catch. The fishing port with its *criée* (fish auction) and the Centre Nautique are on the right immediately as you descend to the town. Ahead lies the natural curving *sillon* which encloses the pleasure-craft harbour. In the little back streets you will discover that Camaret is also a centre for artists of many kinds, with galleries freely open to visitors.

Next door to the tourist office, the **Maison du Patrimoine** ⓘ *Jun-Sep Mon-Sat 1400-1800*, every afternoon Jul and Aug, presents many aspects of the marine history of the area. For those not technically minded, the attraction of this workaday display is in the small details, like needles for the making and mending of nets, and fishermen's footwear, conjuring up a former way of life.

Tour Vauban ⓘ *Apr-end Sep Tue-Sun 1400-1700, Jul and Aug daily 1400-1800, plus 1000-1200, €3.*
This distinctive terracotta-coloured tower was built under Vauban's auspices not a moment too soon. It saw action in 1694, successfully fending off an English attack that ended disastrously for the invaders (a nearby beach is called La Morte Anglaise). The displays inside the tower illustrate famous examples of Vauban's work in northern Finistère, and a

vaulted guardroom has reconstruction paintings of the English offensive. The little marine church of Rocamadour nearby lost the top of its tower to an English cannonball in the same onslaught.

Alignments of Lagatjar/Manoir de Coecilian → *For listings, see pages 47-49.*

Above Camaret on the way to the Pointe de Penhir is the Neolithic alignment of Lagatjar, where 143 stones form three lines, many others having been lost. Birdwatchers, keep your eyes open – there are often choughs to be seen around here. Just visible on the cliff top opposite are the towers of the Manoir de Coecilian. This eerie ruin was a noted centre of culture as the house of poet St-Pol-Roux. In 1940 German soldiers burst in and attacked the old man and his daughter after killing their servant. He died soon after and the house was bombed by Allied aircraft.

Musée de la Bataille de l'Atlantique → *For listings, see pages 47-49.*

ⓘ *On the road between Camaret and the Pointe de Penhir, T02-98 27 92 58. Jul and Aug 1000-1200, 1400-1800, Easter, Jun, Sep 1400-1800. €4.*
Situated in a coastal old bunker, part of the Mur de l'Atlantique or Atlantic Wall, this museum tells the story of the conflict at sea between German and Allied forces, as submarines sought to destroy the supply ships that kept England going. It is a sobering and moving view of terrible loss and destruction. Churchill recognized that this struggle was a crucial factor in the war – 'we must never forget that everything depended on its outcome'.

The **Pointe de Penhir**, nearby, has a huge memorial to the Breton resistance and, beyond, a string of rocks known as the Tas de Pois (pile of peas) stretches out into the ocean.

Morgat and around → *For listings, see pages 47-49.*

ⓘ *2 km south of Crozon.*
This idyllic traditional holiday resort with its brightly painted houses was colonized in the 1920s by rich Parisians, whose lavish villas set the style of the surrounding hills. It's perfect for bucket-and-spade activities, with sweets, waffles and nougat stalls taking the place of candyfloss, or water sports. Boats leave from the port here for visits to the extraordinary **marine grottoes** (grottes-morgat.fr).

Not far away is the **Maison des Minéraux** ⓘ *Jul and Aug 1000-1900, May-Jun 1000-1200, 1400-1700, closed Sat, Sep-Apr 1400-1700, closed Sat and Sun at St-Hernot*, which presents the geology of the Crozon Peninsula. Displays of minerals and fossils hold children's interest too, but the biggest treat is the last room where fluorescent crystals are displayed. Wait for the lights to go out!

It's well worth an excursion to the wild west coast to see the remarkable Iron Age fort at **Lostmarc'h**. Those ready to clamber down – with care – to the beach can marvel at the geological oddity of pillow-lavas, which can be seen embedded in white limestone.

The Crozon Peninsula listings

For Sleeping and Eating price codes and other relevant information, see page 13.

🛏 Where to stay

€€ Trouz ar Mor, *Kerloc'h, T02 98 27 83 57, trouzarmor.com*. Perfect for a spot of self-indulgence, this retreat is perched above the fabulous beach of Kerloc'h. The breakfast room and front bedrooms enjoy the lovely view. The bright house has a calm and happy atmosphere. There's a yoga room, large sauna and fitness equipment. Hosts Galya, Frédéric and Karen keep the emphasis on relaxation, with a range of massage treatments available.

€ Hôtel de la Plage, *42 bd de la Plage, Morgat, T02 98 16 02 16, presquile-crozon. com/hotel-de-la-plage*. Good value at this friendly hotel on the seafront, recently refurbished. The first-floor restaurant has panoramic views, and a bar terrace across the road allows you to sip your drinks beachside. Book in advance to be sure of getting a room with a sea view.

€ Hôtel Styvel, *2 quai de Styvel, Camaret, T02 98 27 92 74, camaret-sur-mer.com/ les-hotels-residences-et-plein.php*. Open all year. Excellent position for this hotel/ restaurant overlooking the sea and Tour Vauban. Try to get a room in the front, not only for the views but to avoid the noise of the kitchen at the back. No 2 is the nicest, with a good-sized bathroom. You won't be disappointed with the food at dinner (see restaurants below), and the hotel is good value for money.

Chambres-d'hôtes/self-catering

€ Gîtes-St-Hernot, *St Hernot, T02 98 27 15 00, presquile-crozon.com/gites-saint-hernot*. Invaluable stop, much used by walkers as it is not far off the coastal path. Jacqueline Le Guillou, a characterful host, offers *chambres d'hôtes* and a *gîte d'étape* (very basic, about €16 a night) behind the bar-restaurant in this little village. The three letting bedrooms are in an apartment which can be rented as one unit. Kitchen facilities are available, but the restaurant is excellent value, and one of the packed lunches will keep you going all day along the cliffs.

L'Ancrage, *Kergalet, Lanvéoc, T02 98 17 01 31, brittanysail.co.uk*. Open Apr-Sep. Richard and Sue Curtis have two *gîtes* (sleeping six and two to three) at their sailing school base near Crozon, and a family home (for eight) to let at Camaret. The gîtes are in outbuildings converted to a very high standard. The larger one has bedrooms downstairs and a living room above to take advantage of the country views. Guests are welcome to share the peaceful gardens. Prices range from €350-475 for two, and €450-595 for six.

Camping

Camping Plage de Trez Rouz, *Camaret, T02 98 27 93 96, trezrouz.com. Open mid-Mar to mid-Oct*. Superb position for this pleasant site, by the 'Red Beach', so called for its striking cliff colour (or for English blood from 1694, according to gorier versions). There are good facilities and children's activities. Mobile homes have terraces with sea views and a rental of about €310 for four people in late June or early September.

🍴 Restaurants

€€ Le Langoustier, *1 esplanade Jim Sevellec, Camaret, T02 98 27 99 00. Daily Apr-Sep, lunch and dinner*. Many dishes here are distinctively herb flavoured, so wafts of rosemary, thyme and garlic follow servers out to the terrace overlooking the *sillon*. Try the meltingly delicious tuna steak or pork fillet with vanilla sauce. The lunchtime menu *du pêcheur*, with a starter/dessert and fish of the day is a bargain. The restaurant is extremely popular, so get there early.

€€ Restaurant – Hôtel Styvel, *2 quai de Styvel, Camaret, T02 98 27 92 74. Daily lunch* and dinner. You can eat in the dining room with its nautical-themed paintings, or out on the terrace here. The emphasis is naturally on fish and shellfish, although there are a few meaty options, such as duck. One perfectly balanced main course is salmon and pollack in a light cream herb sauce, served with potato stack and delicate carrot flan.

€€ Saveurs et Marée, *52 bd de la Plage, . Morgat, T02 98 26 23 18, saveurs-et-maree. com. Open 1200-1400, 1900-2200, Oct-Mar closed Mon and Tue.* In the heart of the town with great sea views, this restaurant offers fishy delights, in soup, salad or starring role. Lobster and choucroutrie de mer are specialities, but there are other options such as veal and duck.

€ Goustadig, *Landévennec, T06 15 71 10 20. Mid-Jun to mid-Sep, otherwise Sun and school holidays.* A cheap and cheerful salon du thé and crêperie by the old abbey, with rustic decor, simple well-cooked food and a good atmosphere. The menu is basically a 'create your own' format from lists of sweet and savoury fillings, but with suggestions like goat's cheese with home-made green tomato chutney and Roquefort with blackberry jam. Preserves are the house speciality.

€ Le Korrigan Crêperie, *Route de Postolonnec, Morgat, T02 98 27 14 37, creperie-le-korrigan-crozon.fr. Jul and Aug daily, Sep-Jun closed Mon.* A fabulous setting for this crêperie overlooking the bay, and a large outdoor terrace to make the most of it and watch the seagulls wheeling over the water as you eat. The eponymous crêpe has goat's cheese, Roquefort and nuts with a green salad; La Peskette is packed with smoked salmon and chives in a cream sauce. Service and food are excellent.-

Cafés and bars

Café du Port, *Morgat.* This little café/bar is around the curve of the beach towards the port, so not quite so frenetically busy in summer as many others. Its small terrace is a pleasant place to sit and watch activity in the bay.

O Shopping

Clothes

Armor Lux, *Route de Camaret, T02 98 26 27 90. Summer hours Mon-Sat 1000-1930, otherwise Mon-Fri 1000-1230, 1400-1830, Sat 1000-1230, 1400-1900.* Just outside Crozon, this outlet of the best-known Breton clothing retailer has a large shop, also selling regional products.

Sports equipment

Absolute Surf, *4 rue Kreisker, Morgat, T02 98 17 01 96. Mon-Sat 1000-1300, 1500-1900, Sun pm only, irregular hours out of season.* Buy or hire water sports gear and equipment. It is also the contact point for the Ecole de Surf (surfing school).

▲ What to do

Peninsula le Labyrinthe, *Route de Dinan, Crozon, T02 98 26 25 34, peninsulalabyrinthe. com. Jul and Aug daily 1000-1900, Apr-Jun and Sep daily 1400-1800, Oct-Mar Wed, Sat, Sun and national holidays 1400-1800, €7/6.* Humorous and well-planned entertainment designed for children, but fun for adults too: a wooden panel maze with story-board clues. Exhibition about mazes and games for youngsters too.

Diving

Presqu'ilemersion diving school (T06 18 05 91 76, presquilemersion.com), based in Crozon, is open all year round for exploring the rocky coastline of the peninsula. Novices and experienced divers can enjoy face-to-face encounters with the extraordinary inhabitants of the underwater world in all their weird and wonderful colours and shapes. Equipment can be hired, professional diving instructors accompany and an initiation session costs from €45. Courses for children are also available.

Horse riding

Whether you want to learn to ride in beautiful surroundings or simply enjoy a day on horseback around the lanes, Les **Petites Ecuries** (T06 62 87 13 09, les-petites-ecuries.chez-alice.fr) in Crozon welcomes visitors all year round. They offer an outing of one or two hours by the sea for novices or experienced riders. At the land end of the peninsula, the **Ferme Equestre de Neiscaouen** (T02 98 27 37 11) near Landévennec offers similar options. Phone in advance to make arrangements.

Sailing

Brittany Sail (brittanysail.co.uk), a RYA-recognized sailing school, offers sailing on their yacht, *Cornish Legend*, with as much or as little active participation as you require. For those who want qualifications, there are courses for beginners and serious sailors. The Competent Crew course covers simple manoeuvres, and the Day Skipper course (over five days) concentrates on seamanship, navigation and pilotage. Richard Curtis has been sailing in these waters for 30 years and will introduce you (and non-sailing partners along for the cruise) to the Rade de Brest and the Atlantic islands of Sein, Molène and Ouessant.

Accommodation is available in gîtes – see Where to stay, page 47.

Walking

The coastal path (GR34 – red and white waymarks) gives access to some of the most spectacular walking in Brittany. If you can manage the logistics of linear walking, this is more satisfying than circuits through the not-particularly-attractive interior. An exception to this is at Landévennec, where the forest provides some lovely paths. Much of the northern coast around Lanvéoc and the Ile-Longue submarine station is off-limits for military security. The best walking is from Camaret to Morgat, a distance of about 40 km, making a fantastic two-day hike, but if you have less time or inclination, the short walk (6 km) from Camaret to the Pointe de Penhir has unbeatable sea views. Continuing to the wonderful sands of Kerloc'h doubles the distance, but you can return along quiet roads directly to Camaret.

The wildest walking is the 10 km from the Pointe de Dinan through Lostmar'ch to the Cap de la Chèvre, an unforgettable route where you will feel alone in the world outside July and August. The *gîte d'étape* for walkers at St-Hernot (see Where to stay, page 47) is easily accessible from the east or west coasts.

Water sports

For a whole variety of water sports, equipment hire and tuition, the **Centre Nautique de Crozon-Morgat** (T02 98 16 00 00, cncm.fr) is open throughout the year, with points on the beach and at the port in Morgat. You can enjoy the safe waters of the Bay of Morgat or Bay of Douarnenez for sailing (including motor and catarmaran), surfing and windsurfing, or why not learn to kitesurf? Sea-kayaking (single or double seat) can also be arranged at any time of the year. What a great, hands-on way to discover the fabulous marine grottoes of Morgat!

Douarnenez and Cap Sizun

The energetic town of Douarnenez, with its popular boat museum, is the gateway to Cap Sizun and the Pointe du Raz, one of the westernmost tips of France and an area of steep cliffs and dramatic Atlantic seascapes. It's a great choice for exhilarating coastal walking or cycling on small roads, with the Goyen estuary and Goulien reserve attracting many birdwatchers. For a rural contrast, picturesque Locronan, a location much in demand for film sets, is just inland.

Douarnenez → *For listings, see page 53.*

This is an energetic town of three ports: Rosmeur, the working fishing harbour, Treboul, packed with pleasure boats, and in between, the living boat museum of Port de Rhu. **Le Port-Musée** (port-musee.org) ① *Jul and Aug daily 1000-1900, Apr-Jun, Sep-Oct 1000-1230, 1400-1800, closed Mon, €7.50*, is a fascinating, colourful collection of boats and boating paraphernalia. Outside on the water are further examples, which visitors can explore.

The history of Douarnenez is dominated by the humble sardine. Disappearance of stocks in the bay between 1902 and 1912 caused enormous hardship, forcing the local fishermen to adapt to new ways to fill the gap. 1924 saw a famous strike by sardine workers at the Usine Carnaud over appalling pay and conditions – social action has always been a feature of the town which elected the first communist mayor in France in 1921.

The green oasis of the **Plomarc'h**, which inspired artists such as Renoir and Boudin, has the remains of traditional workers' hamlets, a community farm with animals on show and a Roman factory where garum, a fish sauce, was made and exported. There are also fine views of the Bay of Douarnenez where the island of Ys, the Breton Atlantis, was traditionally situated.

The **tourist office** ① *T02 98 92 13 35, douarnenez-tourisme.com*, in Rue Dr Mével has walking trails of the town. The market is held in the square here on Mondays, but fresh produce is available daily from Les Halles, the covered market.

Locronan → *For listings, see page 53.*

① *10 km east of Douarnenez.*

Picturesque Locronan (sacred place of Ronan) has been the backdrop for many films, including Roman Polanski's *Tess*. The fine houses are a reflection of wealth brought to the town by the manufacture of sailcloth, first mentioned in 1469.

Locronan has long been associated with the creative arts and there are still many artisans working here today – in sculpture, ceramics, glassware and art.

Carved on the pulpit in the great church you can see the eventful story of St-Ronan, who first set up his oratory in the Bois du Nevet, site of a former Celtic *nemeton* or sacred grove of nature deities. He christianized this into a 12-km circuit representing the months of the Celtic year. Every six years (the next time is in 2013) La Grande Troménie is held – a celebratory walk around the 12 'stations', but each year there's a Petite Troménie in July.

Cap Sizun → *For listings, see page 53.*

Pointe du Millier

This point, with its lighthouse, has glorious views, but on the way you should divert into the woods to see the Moulin de Keriolet with an 8-m working wheel. The stream has a mini 'chaos' of granite boulders, and if you step across them and up the bank opposite you will see the stone boat in which Saint Conogan arrived on these shores (allegedly).

Pointe du Van

This promontory is less busy than the Pointe du Raz opposite, but just as beautiful. The **Chapelle de St-They** honours a sixth-century monk from Great Britain. According to local legend, the chapel bell rings spontaneously to warn sailors of danger.

Don't miss the breathtakingly beautiful **Baie des Trépassés** (Bay of the Dead) nearby.

Pointe du Raz

The visitor centre (required parking €6) is set 500 m back from the point to preserve the natural splendour of one of the most visited sites in France. It's a pity about the hideous statue of the Virgin overlooking the sea. This is not quite the most westerly point of France, but the rocky heights are impressive. Offshore, the almost flat Ile de Sein is usually visible.

Cycling tour

This is quite a demanding route of 44 km around Cap Sizun starting from the harbour of Audierne. You'll enjoy pretty chapels, spectacular seascapes and the memorable Baie des Trépassés between the Pointe du Raz and Pointe du Van. (For an easier option, ride up the Goyen estuary to pretty Pont-Croix and back, a total distance of about 12km.)

From the centre of Audierne bear right along the harbour towards the Embarcadère. Before that, just past the little chapel of St-Evette, turn right at a mini-roundabout uphill through old houses. At the top, follow right towards the *bourg* and then through the hamlets of Kerhoun, Creac'h, Brignéoc'h and Keromen. After this, turn left at a junction and proceed via Custrein to the **Chapelle de Tugen**.

This exceptional chapel (c 1550) in its walled enclosure has a 28-m tower and elaborately decorated interior. The saint is invoked against rabies and the rabid pain of toothache.

Keep to left of the chapel (signed Pointe du Raz) and continue uphill, bearing left and ahead towards the *bourg* of **Primelin**. At a fork, go right towards the centre. Keep left of the church, then turn left to the hamlet of Kermaléro. Just after it, turn right at the crossroads. At the next junction, go ahead to join the main road (the D784), turning left to cross Le Loc'h.

Continue uphill for 100 m (past two turns) then turn very sharp left, signed to Keringar. Go straight through, then turn off left (as the road bends right) through Toramor and on uphill. Where the road splits, either go right to rejoin the main road (500 m ahead) or first divert left uphill for 475 m to the **Chapelle de Notre-Dame du Bon Voyage**, situated on a high viewpoint. This chapel has seats and a picnic table nearby.

At the main road (the D784) turn left and continue to **Plogoff**, which has a bakery and refreshments. Carry on along the same road past the tiny chapel of St-Yves on the left. Continue through Kerguidy and past the **Biscuiterie** (in case you're hungry). Then turn right (the D607), signed Baie des Trépassés.

Diversion: go straight on (2 km) to see the natural splendour of the Pointe du Raz, then return.

Descend steeply on the D607 to the Etang de Laoual and the magnificent **Baie des Trépassés** (Bay of the Dead).

Diversion: to see the Chapelle St-Tugdual with its fontaine and lavoir in a pretty setting, follow the main road on for 200 m, then branch right and continue for 1 km.

Turn left just before the Relais Hotel and go up a narrow, very steep road all the way to the top – your reward will be spectacular views!

At the top, go left and then follow round right to a T-junction. Then go left to the **Chapelle St-They** and on round to the **Point du Van** (or right for information, toilets and seasonal *café* first).

St-They was a sixth-century monk who came from Great Britain. The T of his name has mutated from D (Dei) – in Cornwall his name is St Day. Return and take the D7 heading east (in the direction of Douarnenez).

Diversion: after 1 km, turn left to Castelmeur (800 m). This peninsula was fortified in the Iron Age, as weapons found here show. The defensive system consisted of four banks and three ditches. Excavation revealed 95 habitations on the slopes behind, indicated by patches of greener vegetation.

Continue on the D7 (past the windmill on the left) for 1.5 km and turn right (on a left bend), signed Poulc'haradeg.

Diversion: for the 40-ha Réserve du Cap Sizun continue ahead on the D7 for 5 km and then turn left where signed. Choughs, shags, fulmars, razorbills and many others make their homes here.

Go right at the split immediately after, on a single-track road, and left 1 km later at a T-junction. Continue to Cléden-Cap-Sizun, visible across a little valley. Then carry on ahead (on the D43) for 1.5 km to Quivillic. The **Chapelle de Langroas** is 300 m beyond on the roadside, by a stream and picnic table. Go straight on through Lezoualc'h (past a superb manor house with a stair turret on the right).

Diversion: 1 km later, go left for 350 m to Goulien, where the church has Celtic stele in its precinct, and nearby is the Maison du Vent, interpretation centre for the wind farm nearby.

Continue for 1.5 km through Kervoen.

Diversion: turn left (on a right-hand bend) for diversion (600 m) to the isolated Chapelle St-Laurent with an unusual triangular calvary, and a menhir nearby.

Continue 800 m to Les Quatre Vents, and turn right (the D43A), signed **Audierne**, and return there via a roundabout at Esquibien.

Douarnenez and Cap Sizun listings

For Sleeping and Eating price codes and other relevant information, see page 13.

● Where to stay

€€ Hôtel de la Baie des Trépassés, *Plogoff, T02 98 70 61 34, hotelfinistere.com.* A superb location right on the beach of this bay at the end of the world. Sleep in a comfortable room facing the ocean, with the sound of the waves breaking gently outside – it's great for a romantic break or for walking the coastal path. The hotel also has a decent restaurant with that priceless view.

● Restaurants

Douarnenez *p51*
€€-€ Chez Fanch, *49 rue Anatole France, T02 98 92 31 77, chez-fanch.com. Jul and Aug daily 1200-1400, 1900-2200, Sep-Jun closed Thu.* Breton flags, multilingual menus and whimsical drawings greet you on arrival. Just a few paces up from the port, the restaurant has a very attractive interior, with roaring fire in winter. Set menus from €11.90-44 are excellent value, with good choice. The soupe de poissons is a flavoursome starter.

€€-€ La Trinquette, *29 quai du Grand Port, T02 98 92 11 10. Open 1200-1400, 1900-2130, closed in winter.* As you'd expect in the town's fishing port area, a fish menu with everything fresh. Maybe start with rillettes of sardines dressed with balsamic vinegar, followed by a thick tuna steak in chilli tomato sauce with saffron rice. Prawns, scallops and oysters also feature on a changing menu of specials, according to supply.

Cafés and bars

Le Mercure bar (T02 98 74 02 64) in the Tréboul port area is popular with young people in the evening; likewise **Les Docks** (bd Jean Richepin, T02 98 92 21 95) and **Le Banana Boat** (47 quai du Port Rhu, T02 98 92 10 43).

● Shopping

Douarnenez *p51*
Penn Sardin, *7 rue Le Breton, T02 98 92 70 83, pennsardin.com. Open 0930-1200, 1430-1900, closed Tue out of season.* A truly Breton experience, the sardine shop! Superb products and decorative tins.

Morlaix and the Monts d'Arrée

Morlaix, with its attractive pleasure port, is dominated by the viaduct of the Paris–Brest railway, soaring above the medieval heart below. It's the first stop for those off the ferry at Roscoff eager for French coffee and provisions. Nearby is a collection of the best parish closes, a Breton phenomenon mostly found here in the district of Léon. The border between that and Cornouaille is the range of the Monts d'Arrée, the highest hills of Brittany, a special landscape positively oozing with legends and historical gems.

Morlaix → For listings, see pages 59-60.

The town has a fabulous food market on Saturday mornings in the Place Allende, and shoppers will also enjoy the cobbled streets of chic shops in half-timbered buildings. It's an atmospheric place squashed into a deep river valley, with a pleasure port alongside impressive buildings of a former tobacco factory, now being revitalized for cultural use. Above all this is the distinctive pink granite **viaduct**, 60 m high and 292 m long, constructed during the 1860s for the new Paris–Brest railway. It dwarfs the Flamboyant-Gothic **Eglise St-Melaine** (1489) which overlooks the Place des Otages and fine **town hall**. The square commemorates 60 hostages taken by the Germans in reprisal for an attack on an officers' mess. They were deported to Buchenwald, and few returned after the war.

Explore the old town via the *venelles*, stepped passageways criss-crossing three hillsides. The tourist office (on the steps opposite the church of St-Melaine) has a map of routes. Morlaix lost its castle after the Wars of Religion – sadly there's now a bungalow on the spot, but you can climb the steep steps from the Rue de Mur for wonderful views from the little park.

Browse the antique and antiquarian bookshops in the old Quartier de St-Mathieu around **Eglise St-Mathieu** with its original tower of 1584. This attractive church with a restored barrel-vaulted ceiling contains an unusual wooden statue of the Virgin (Notre-Dame du Mur), dating from 1390.

The best of the medieval houses are to be found in **Rue Ange de Guernisac** and **Grand'Rue**, where a superlative example is open to the public (see below). There are also remains of the walls of the *ville close* in Rue de l'Hospice, where there's a picture of the church that once dominated the area with the tallest spire in the region – it fell down in 1806 after stone was removed to sell for building material.

Musée de Morlaix

① *T02 98 88 68 88, musee.ville.morlaix.fr. Jul and Aug 1000-1230, 1400-1830, Sep-Oct and Apr-May 1000-1200, 1400-1800, Sun 1400-1800, closed Mon, Nov-Mar and Jun 1000-1200, 1400-1700, closed Mon and Sun. €4.10, family €6.60.*
This is currently a split site between Les Jacobins, with changing exhibitions, and No 9 Grand'Rue, a superb 16th-century house. There may be a move to the old tobacco factory on the quay in a few years.

Place des Jacobins

The Jacobins church (not open to the public) is the oldest building in Morlaix. The monastery housed many famous guests such as Anne de Bretagne and Mary Queen of Scots, who arrived as a child in 1548, after a dreadful sea crossing on her way to engagement with the Dauphin. Changing art exhibitions are held here in the adjoining halls.

No 9 Grand'Rue

In a narrow cobbled street, this is an example of a unique architectural type called *maison à pondalez*, from *pont* (bridge) and *aller* (to go). The towering central space with a monumental fireplace rises through four floors with wooden 'bridges' off to each side of an amazingly carved central turning wooden stair. High-quality items of Breton furniture, paintings and panels presenting the history of Morlaix are well displayed. Houses of this kind were urban châteaux for nobles turned merchants in quest of wealth, often in the linen trade which employed thousands in this region. Highly recommended for a visit.

The so-called **House of the Duchess Anne** ① *May-Sep 1100-1800, 1830 Jul and Aug, closed Sun,* in similar style, in the Place Allende, is also open to the public.

Monts d'Arrée → *For listings, see pages 59-60.*

Of these, the highest hills in Brittany, **Roc'h Ruz** (near the transmissions mast) is the topmost point at just over 385 m. Until recent, accurate measurements, **Roc'h Trevezel** was deemed the tallest, unless you count the spire of the little chapel of St-Michel-de-Brasparts, whose silhouette dominates views further west. You can drive up almost to the top of this Mont St-Michel and enjoy panoramic views of Finistère, but particularly of the *landes* (moors) and *tourbières* (peat marsh) which characterize this area. The near view includes the reservoir and first nuclear power station in France (long since decommissioned).

Granite has eroded in this exposed chain of hills and the remaining crags are formed of a mixture of schist and quartzite. The wilderness of the landscape has an eerie appeal and, when the mist lies thickly over the low ground like a silver lake with sharp crags of schist jutting above, it's not hard to understand why it has become a place of legend. The name of a nearby hamlet, Youdig, means 'little porridge', reflecting the dangers of being sucked down into the marsh. The entrance to the Celtic underworld was thought to be here in the Yeun Ellez, and Ankou's spirit looms large. Tales tell of a huge black dog roaming the marshes and, more bizarrely, nocturnal washerwomen calling travellers to help with laundry baskets, thus luring them to their deaths. A line of standing stones known as The Wedding Party wends its way through the heather, said to be drunken revellers petrified by an angry priest who tried to pass them.

Moulins de Kerouat

① *2 km west of Commana, via D764. T02 98 68 87 76, ecomusee-monts-arree.fr. Jul and Aug daily 1100-1900, mid-Mar to May, Sep-Oct Mon-Fri 1000-1800, Sun 1400-1800, Jun 1000-1800, Sat and Sun 1400-1800. €4.50/2.10.*

Set in a peaceful green valley, this eco-museum vividly presents the atmosphere of simple life in rural Brittany from the 17th to 19th centuries. There are waterwheels, mill-machinery and a tannery, with outbuildings containing exhibitions and artefacts that bring home the harsh realities of economic life in the Monts d'Arrée. Don't miss the wonderful examples of huge carved grain chests and box beds.

Maison Cornec

① *St-Rivoal, via D30/D42. T02 98 81 40 99, ecomusee-monts-arree.fr, Jul and Aug 1100-1900, Jun 1400-1800, €1.50/1.*

Dating from 1702, this house is in a style called *maison anglaise*, with an exterior stone staircase and protruding gable that provided an important extra living space (the family shared the ground floor with their animals). Various paths go around the grounds, preserved in their old form, passing a *lavoir* and little river in the bottom of the valley.

The enlos paroissial is a phenomenon particularly linked to northern Finistère. It arose out of an increase in wealth in the 16th and 17th centuries, thanks largely in the region of Léon to the linen trade with England. Farmers, weavers and merchants put their money into grandiose expressions of faith and pride rather than individual ostentation. Thus small villages came to have huge and elaborate churches, with rivalry between different communities leading to outrageously competitive building and decoration.

The ingredients of this mini city of God are the church, calvary, ossuary for the bones of the dead and an encircling precinct, originally containing the cemetery, with symbolic triumphal entrance. The same basic elements make up each parish close, but there is a huge degree of variation and presentation from church to church. Three of the best known are in close proximity and generally open to visitors every day, except when services are taking place.

St-Thégonnec
ⓘ *12 km southwest of Morlaix.*

Built mostly between 1587 and 1682, this most grandiose of parish closes is exuberant in form and feeling. It is dedicated to the sixth-century Welsh monk Conog (Breton form Tegoneg). The legend goes that a wolf killed the stag that was pulling Conog's cart full of building stones so the monk forced the wolf to take the stag's place. This appears in iconography here on the porch and calvary and again inside.

Through the stolid triumphal gate, the verticality of the overall design is striking – everything points symbolically upwards. The church oddly has two towers, one the remnant of a former structure, and the main one, built in competition with that of Pleyben, another fine *enclos*. The ossuary is encircled by an inscription, the key words being *'hodie mihi, cras tibi'* (I die today, you will tomorrow). Inside in the crypt a *mise en tombeau* scene has amazingly expressive mourning faces.

The calvary (1610), shows 40 figures in nine scenes of the Passion, from Jesus' arrest to his Resurrection. There is a marked contrast between brutish faces (like the idiot with the lolling tongue), showing the ugliness of sin, and the serenity of the women, secure in their faith. Contemporary fashion detail can be gleaned from the costumes, such as the rounded hats. The cross shows angels taking the sacred blood of Christ, origin of the Holy Grail legend.

Inside the church the glorious density of ornamentation captures the attention. A fire in 1998 badly damaged the interior – a display of charred remains near the organ shows the extent of the restoration project – so cleaning and repainting have vivified the altarpieces and statuary. In the north transept is a Retable du Rosaire with a statue of Saint Louis IX, king of France, because the altar was ordered on the saint's day. Adam and Eve, driven from Eden, are shown, with Purgatory and the fires of hell graphically displayed. The main figures are the Virgin Mary, with Ste-Catherine to one side and St-Dominic on the other. The little dog with a torch in his mouth is a word-play symbol – the Latin *Dominicani* separates into *domini cani* (dogs of the Lord) guarding the faith.

Guimiliau
ⓘ *16 km southwest of Morlaix.*

A beautiful ensemble here, but it's the calvary (1581) that draws visitors from all over the world. More than 200 figures are depicted in a medieval fashion parade. In addition to the usual scenes of the Passion and Resurrection, there is a graphic scene of the naked figure of Katel Gollet (Mad Kate) being gobbled up by the monsters of hell. Details on the frieze include the tender image of Mary touching her baby's foot on the flight into Egypt, and Veronica holding up her handkerchief with an image of Christ. There are many little touches of realism, like Jesus' rolled-up sleeve as he washes the disciples' feet, or the Last Supper showing hungry disciples and Judas with a bulging purse.

The façade of the south porch (1606-1617) has numerous carvings illustrating Old Testament scenes, such as Adam and Eve's fall and a delightful little vignette of Noah's Ark. Inside the porch is a fine collection of the Twelve Apostles, each with their special attribute. The small frieze below contains some oddities – the birth of Eve with God pulling her from Adam's rib, and the 'Cock King', in reference to a medieval cock-fighting ritual.

The interior boasts an exceptional organ (c1690) by Englishman Thomas Dallam, whose family fled to Brittany from Cromwell's Puritanism. Nearby are two remarkably preserved 17th-century processional banners (carried in the pardon) in glass cases, one with St-Miliau, patron of this church.

His story is told in an altarpiece to the right of the main altar area. This sixth-century saint, once ruler of Cornouaille, was beheaded on orders of his jealous brother Rivoad. There's a poignant image of the saint holding his own head, supported by his wife.

The Altarpiece of St Joseph commemorates a royal decree of 1661, setting a public holiday for St Joseph. Above the main image of Joseph holding his son Jesus by the hand, is St-Laurent shown carrying his own portable barbecue. He was martyred by being roasted alive, allegedly calling out to his torturers to turn him over because one side was done. Below is the lawyer St-Yves, patron saint of Brittany, conventionally shown between a rich and a poor man, symbolizing his fairness of judgement.

Lampaul-Guimiliau

ⓘ 19 km southwest of Morlaix.

This enclos has a relatively simple exterior with a narrow triumphal entrance, plain calvary, and ossuary with a superb doorway interestingly uniting a Tree of Life with the inscription momento mori. The truncated bell tower (1573) was one of the highest in Brittany until lightning struck in 1809. An ornate Gothic entry porch, with a good set of Apostle statues, is a taste of things to come, for the interior of this church, dedicated to St-Miliau and St-Pol (Paul Aurelien), is most impressive.

At the rear is a mise en tombeau scene of exceptional quality in touffeau, with each figure lost in their own emotions. Mary looks on in suppressed anguish as John offers wordless comfort; a greater complexity of feelings is shown on the face of Mary Magdalene. Next to this are two remarkable processional banners surviving from the 17th century and, opposite, is a bright baroque baptistery (1650) in octagonal form, which has a riot of details from twisting vines to mini-statues of the Apostles and Christ's own baptism.

The nave is dominated by its glowingly decorative poutre de gloire (beam of glory) with scenes from the Passion on one side and the Annunciation on the other, a poignant contrast. Ahead, the main altarpieces are of John the Baptist and the Passion. Here, a highly elaborate display shows Miliau decapitated by his brother, holding his own head. On the left, there's a rare depiction – Anne resting in bed having given birth to the Virgin Mary, while midwives wash the baby. The patron saint of Brittany has her own altarpiece on the north wall. Another female saint, Margaret, is also honoured on the south. Punished for her faith, she was swallowed by a dragon, but she used her cross to scratch his stomach and he coughed her up. She became the patron of childbirth, as mothers prayed for such an easy delivery.

Morlaix and the Monts d'Arrée listings

For Sleeping and Eating price codes and other relevant information, see page 13.

🛏 Where to stay

Morlaix *p55*

€€€ Le Manoir de Coat Amour, *Route de Paris, T02 98 88 57 02, www.gites-morlaix. com*. The name Coat Amour (Wood of Love) lends an appropriately romantic air here. Bed and breakfast in palatial rooms is available at this impressive manoir. It's a short walk to the restaurants in town, but an evening meal is available if booked in advance. There are luxurious gîtes in the gorgeous gardens. The units (one for six or seven, the other for two) have everything for a relaxing holiday in this oasis of calm. Outdoor swimming pool in summer. Small gîte €425-775, large gîte €700-1400.

€€ Hôtel du Port, *3 quai de Léon, T02 98 88 07 54, lhotelduport.com*. Great value for this super-friendly hotel, very popular with British visitors. It's situated by the river in the centre of Morlaix, perfectly placed for restaurants and sights. Rooms are simply decorated with good facilities like plasma TV and internet access (Wi-Fi). Jean-Christophe Rollet and his team are rightly proud of their welcoming establishment.

Monts d'Arrée *p56*

€€ Chambres d'hôtes de Brézéhant, *Lac du Drennec, T02 98 78 02 32, chambres-hotes-brezehant.fr*. This gem of a place is in the heart of the Monts d'Arrée and very near Lac du Drennec with its swimming beaches. The 17th-century weaver's house is full of original art and choice furniture, as you'd expect in the home of a professional artist and potter. The guests' sitting room has a huge ancient fireplace, and bedrooms are strikingly individual. Andréas and Catherine Merényi will be happy to advise on things to see and do in the area.

🍴 Restaurants

Morlaix *p55*

€€ L'Estaminet, *23 rue du Mur, T02 98 88 00 17, restaurantmorlaix.com. 1200-1400 and 1900-2200, closed Wed*. Once you get used to sitting in a leather armchair to eat, you'll appreciate the comfort and stylish decor of this café/brasserie. Service is attentive, the food of chef Patrice Cabioch original and full of fresh tastes. There are diverse specials such as entrecôte steak or fish-stuffed chilli peppers with orange pepper sauce. Salads are fabulous. Highly recommended.

€€-€ La Terrasse, *31 Place des Otages, T02 98 88 20 25. Mon-Sat 1200-1400, 1930-2130, closed Sun*. La Terrasse is very popular with British visitors just off the ferry at Roscoff, but it's hard to get a consensus on the quality of the food and service, as both are variable. Steak and chips is reliably good. The belle epoque decor inside is definitely worth seeing, however, with a wrought-iron staircase, huge mirrors and murals. People-watching from the terrace is the best fun here.

€ Cheese & Co, *13 Place des Otages, T02 98 63 18 49. Tue-Sat 0930-1930, Sun 1000-1300 (evening Fri and Sat, reservation only)*. Near the tourist office, this superb delicatessen specializing in cheese also offers a light but elegant menu, such as tartines or a plate of cold meat with cheese of choice. Jérôme Grill is passionate about his products and you'll appreciate his skill when stocking up with ingredients for your picnic. Nice stop for a coffee too.

€ Crêperie Hermine, *35 rue Ange de Guernisac, T02 98 88 10 91, restaurantmorlaix. com. Mon-Sat 1200-1400, 1900-2130 (Fri and Sat 2200), Sun 1200-1330, 1900-2130*. Perhaps the most popular crêperie in town, with a wide menu and efficient service in one of Morlaix's ancient houses. The seafood speciality fillings are fresh from Roscoff, and you can become better acquainted with some of Brittany's 600+ varieties of seaweed, which make a surprisingly tasty contribution to many kinds of fish and shellfish.

€ Enchanted Crêpe, *26 rue Ange de Guernisac, T02 98 88 69 59. Jul-Aug daily, Sep-Jun Tue-Sat 1200-1400, 1900-2200.* This place suffers unfairly from being too near the long-established Hermine, but our preference is for the unpretentious style and really delicious food found here, whether it's well-filled crêpes, well-cooked steak or plats du terroir. Local sources of ingredients are noted in the menu, which is always a good sign. Friendly service and pleasant atmosphere.

South of Morlaix *p57*
€ Krampouez Breizh Crêperie, *21 place Aristide Briand, Huelgoat, T02 98 99 80 10, creperie-krampouez-breizh.com. Thu-Tue lunch and dinner (Sep-Jun closed Wed evening and Fri).* The best crêperie in town, according to numerous regulars, combining an atmospheric setting in a beautiful old house with Gaelle's friendly service and delicious crêpes. The cheesy fillings are very good here – perhaps Roquefort, Emmenthal and chèvre with walnuts.

€ L'Autre Rive Café/Librairie, *Restidiou Braz, T02 98 99 72 58, autrerive.hautefort. com (blog). Open daily 1100-2100, closed Jan.* A lovely café/bookshop with sofas and internet access, in an idyllic forest setting just outside Huelgoat. Marc is a genial host and the whole atmosphere is relaxed and civilized. A light menu of savoury cake (various flavours made with chestnut flour) and salad, or soup or a cheese/fish/meat plate is available at any time. Yummy ice cream too!

Cafés and bars
Saveurs de Guimiliau, *Guimiliau. Daily 0700-1800, mid-Sep to Easter closed Mon.* This bakery just by the famous parish close has delicious bread and cakes. It also offers tea,

coffee and hot chocolate at outside tables or in a pretty upstairs room. Excellent fare, served by very nice people.

⊙ Shopping

Ferme des Artisans, *nr Mont-St-Michel-de-Brasparts, on D785, T02 98 81 46 69. Jul to mid-Sep daily 1000-1930, mid-Sep to Mar Sat and Sun 1030-1900, Apr-Jun Mon-Fri 1400-1830, Sat-Sun 1030-1900.* A huge shop on two floors with mostly locally produced, good-quality arts and crafts, plus books, jewellery, food and drink, hats, pottery and furniture.

⊙ What to do

Monts d'Arrée *p56*
Horse riding
The **Village Equestre de Bécherel** (T02 98 99 77 24, village-becherel.fr) near Huelgoat offers a day out on horseback (full day €70/half day €45) and/or can teach you how to ride. Special packages with accommodation (gîte) and riding available, from €180 for a weekend.

The **Centre Equestre de Cranou** (T02 98 26 90 27, centre-equestre-du-cranou.com) on the western edge has similar options, plus a *gîte d'étape* and camping.

Walking
The association **ADDES** (T02 98 99 66 58, arree-randos.com) has various guided walks with an emphasis on nature and legends, including one by night (carrying lanterns) on the moors, when you may even meet a korrigan.

Brittany Walks (brittanywalks.com) offers guided walks and tours in English for individuals or families, or advice about walking in the area.

Contents

Côtes d'Armor

Côtes d'Armor contains one of the most famous littoral regions in France – the Pink Granite Coast, with its fantastically shaped rock formations. There are many other equally memorable locations on a coastline that provides the very best in beaches, the highest cliffs in Brittany and plenty of traditional fishing ports. This maritime heritage was encapsulated in the 1990s name change from Côtes du Nord to Côtes d'Armor – Land of the Sea. It's the least populated of Brittany's four departments, but visitor numbers soar in summer around family resorts such as Perros-Guirec.

There are no large cities, but interesting towns in the western half of the department include St-Brieuc, telecommunications centre Lannion and captivating Tréguier, all offering modern facilities against comely historic backdrops.

The interior Argoat is a quieter world, where tiny villages boast lovely chapels and sculpted calvaries, and lofty castles such as Tonquédec and Roch Jagu watch over deep river valleys.

For those in search of energetic holidays, the coast provides a wealth of water sports, while walkers, cyclists and riders cannot fail to be enticed by the incredible variety of unspoilt landscape.

St-Brieuc and the Côte de Goëlo

St-Brieuc sits at the base of a vast bay with one of the largest tidal ranges in the world, causing the seascape to appear remarkably different throughout the day. The Côte de Goëlo is a glorious series of beaches, coves and headlands, where ports and resorts retain a traditional holiday atmosphere. Today, this distinguished, yet often harsh, maritime heritage is celebrated in a series of feasts and festivals.

Walking the coastal path alongside this magnificent bay provides constant visual entertainment, with the most sensational viewing points on the high cliffs around Plouha.

St-Brieuc → *For listings, see pages 68-70.*

St-Brieuc, the administrative capital of Côtes d'Armor, is a labyrinthine old town in two deep valleys of the Gouët and Goëdic. Flying past on the expressway viaducts through an industrial sprawl, there is little sense of what lies below, where the narrow medieval streets are interspersed with lavish 19th-century civic buildings and the brooding presence of a fortress-style **cathedral**. According to legend, St-Brieuc, one of the founding saints of Brittany, arrived here in the fifth century: the site of his earliest settlement is marked by a **fontaine** at the Chapelle Notre-Dame-de-la-Fontaine.

To the north of cathedral lie the best examples of the colourful half-timbered houses. In the Place au Lin, the ornate **Maison Le Ribeault** now houses a restaurant, for dining in cramped historic splendour. Further up the Rue Fardel are fine examples of 16th-century dwellings. No 15, known as the **Hôtel du Chapeau Rouge** or Hôtel des Ducs de Bretagne, is decorated with Renaissance-style sculptures and, at roof-level, a griffon, which became the town's symbol.

In July and August, Les Nocturnes festival livens up the central area, and you can enjoy the spectacle from many bars and restaurants in the heart of the city.

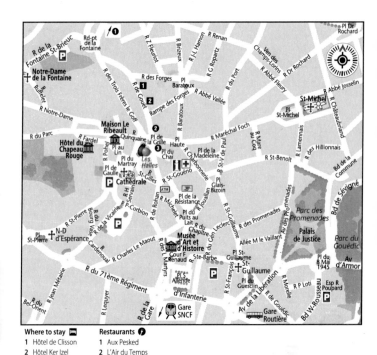

Where to stay
1 Hôtel de Clisson
2 Hôtel Ker Izel

Restaurants
1 Aux Pesked
2 L'Air du Temps
3 La Cuisine du Marché

Cathédrale de St-Etienne
① *Open 1000-1800.*
This sober cathedral still has marks where little shops were once built up against its walls. The high arrow-slits and massive towers, more defensive than aesthetic, are a reminder that the building was besieged during the Wars of Succession. Statues and altarpieces were destroyed at the time of the Revolution, when the cathedral was used as stabling, but the interior is still an impressive sight. The fine altar of St-Sacrament (c 1750), by Yves Corlay, was saved and stands in the south aisle of the nave. In its own little chapel is the tomb of Guillaume Pinchon, the first Breton to be canonized by the church in Rome in 1247. His skull is among the collection of reliquaries of saints nearby.

Le Musée d'Art et d'Histoire
① *Cours Francis Renard, rue des Lycéens Martyrs. Tue-Sat 0930-1145,1330-1745, Sun 1400-1800. Free.*
This is a well-organized town museum. On three floors, the main facets of the 19th-century world of the area are revealed, with maritime replicas and objects at ground level, a well-explained analysis of cloth production with looms and spinning implements on the first floor, and evidence of daily life such as furniture and costumes, including many *coiffes* (distinctive Breton lace headdresses) above. Temporary exhibitions also cover a range of arts and crafts.

Côte de Goëlo → *For listings, see pages 68-70.*

Pointe du Roselier
① *6 km northwest of St-Brieuc.*
Not far from St-Brieuc is this stunning viewpoint for the Côte de Goëlo. There's an orientation table and the *four à boulets*, an elaborate oven where soldiers heated cannonballs to send flying in the direction of English ships prowling the coast below.

Binic
① *14 km northwest of St-Brieuc.*
From the quay of this charming little port you can watch pleasure boats on one side of the jetty and families enjoying the beach on the other. The town has a 'Family Plus' quality mark for its facilities, entertainment and welcoming atmosphere, designed to appeal to all ages. There are many organized events, or you could take a boat up the Goëlo coast to the Ile de Bréhat in summer.

There's a festival to celebrate the cod-fishing tradition in May, with nautical songs and dancing, but now the marine emphasis is on shellfish. The **Museum of Popular Traditions** ① *Apr-end Sep, 1430-1800, closed Tue except in Jul and Aug, €3.50*, is packed with artefacts and models that illuminate the economic and everyday life of the old days.

St-Quay Portrieux
① *22 km northwest of St-Brieuc.*
Visitors today are welcomed a good deal more cordially than Saint Ké, who was beaten by women with gorse twigs on arrival! St-Quay prides itself on being the Coquille St-Jacques (scallop) capital of Brittany, with a festival on that theme in late April or May. There are plenty of eateries to try them at in this family holiday resort (Family Plus mark), with good beaches and summer entertainments. The town blossomed into a popular tourist resort after two ladies from Guingamp tried the curative powers of the seawater baths in

1841, starting a trend which led to rapid development when the railway brought Parisian visitors. A carefully constructed deep-water port, rare on this northern coastline with its tidal peculiarities, keeps this maritime tradition alive. There is a seawater swimming pool on the Plage du Casino for those long low tide times, and the busy Friday market provides another chance to sample fresh local produce.

Palus Plage
ⓘ *28 km northwest of St-Brieuc.*
Don't miss a small sign off the D786 to the simple and unspoilt Palus Plage. Green-clad hills enclose a pebble and sandy crescent, perfect for swimming or just lazing. For the more energetic, the coastal path snakes steeply uphill to the north, giving wonderful views across the bay. There is also a children's playground here and parking for camper vans. Refreshments include a beachside bar in high season, and restaurants by the slipway.

Cliffs of Plouha and Gwin Zegal
Said to be the highest cliffs in Brittany, these undulating verdant hills provide some of the best coastal walking in Côtes d'Armor, with the GR34 footpath running all the way up the Côte de Goëlo. Start from Palus Plage and walk north to Plage Bonaparte, passing many fine viewpoints such as the Point de Plouha (104 m), an up-and-down route of about 8 km. On the way, admire the little harbour of **Gwin Zegal**, where boats are moored to cut-off trunks of trees once planted in the sand with weighted roots. This gave rise to the legend that robbers used to be tied up there and left to the mercy of the tides. Plouha tourist office (T02 96 20 24 73) has a leaflet pack of circular walks in the area.

Plage Bonaparte
ⓘ *4 km from Plouha.*
This was the scene of Operation Bonaparte during 1944, when 135 allied airmen were safely evacuated thanks to a local resistance network, the Réseau Shelburne. '*Bonjour tout le monde à la maison d'Alphonse*' was the coded message for these operations. Brought secretly to a nearby house, the men were then taken to the beach and rowed out to a waiting boat by night. The 'Maison d'Alphonse' was later burnt down by the Germans: its site is marked by a memorial and can be reached by the **Sentier Shelburne**, a footpath off the coast path. La Stèle is a cliff-top memorial to all those involved in this dangerous enterprise. The beach itself is reached through a rocky arch, past another commemorative plaque. It's a popular place for swimming, especially with teenagers in school holidays.

Paimpol
ⓘ *16.5 km northwest of Plouha.*
The modern and rather unattractive port here is now devoted to pleasure craft. The streets of **Vieux Paimpol** branching out from the Place du Martray give a softer impression of the town. The little towered house in the square is where author Pierre Loti used to stay. Rue de l'Eglise leads up to the Vieille Tour (1760), the lonely bell tower of the former parish church. No 5 is an attractive half-timbered house, but even older is 6 Rue des Huit Patriotes, dating from the 15th century, which has been an ironmonger's for more than 100 years.

The town is extremely busy in July and August, when the little **Musée du Costume** ⓘ *1030-1230, 1400-1830, €3,* with Breton furniture and costumes is open, in Rue Raymond Pellier near the tourist office. The **Musée de la Mer** ⓘ *mid-Jun to end Aug 1030-1230, 1400-1830, Apr to mid-Jun and Sep 1400-1800, €5)* is an exhibition underlining the achievements

The strange story of Saint Ké

Saint-Ké, a holy man from Wales, arrived on the shores of Brittany in the sixth century. Suspicious local washerwomen attacked and beat him with gorse branches, leaving Ké bleeding. The Virgin Mary came to his rescue, causing a spring of healing water to gush out of the ground. This is still to be seen, now covered by a later fontaine, near the Grève d'Isnain. Saint-Ké is sometimes identified with Sir Kay of Arthurian legend, and another version of his name lives on in St-Quay Portrieux.

and sacrifices of Paimpol's maritime history, displayed in a former factory with a brick chimney. The town's international sea-shanty festival is in early August.

The best view of the town and bay is from the Tour de Kerroc'h just to the north.

Abbaye de Beauport
ⓘ *Kérity, Paimpol, T02 96 55 18 58, abbaye-beauport.com. Mid-Jun to mid-Sep 1000-1900, Oct-May 1000-1200, 1400-1700. €6.*

The particular quality of this romantic ancient abbey comes from the combination of architecture and environment. Built in a position to profit from natural resources, trade and pilgrimage, it is also scenically a beautiful spot hugging the shore just south of Paimpol. Sudden glimpses of the bay and islands appear through stone arches as you wander around the remains and attractive gardens.

The monks of this Augustine foundation, dating back to the 12th century, later acquired a reputation for dissolute behaviour, hence the saying: *Il n'est de moine à Beauport/ Qui n'ait de femme à Kérity* (There's no monk at Beaufort who hasn't got a woman in Kérity). The size of the church reflects that this was the first continental stopping point for many pilgrims from Britain on the Compostela trail, who were welcomed in the magnificent Salle du Duc. In later centuries it had industrial uses, including cider-making, with a small hydraulic canal still to be seen under a grating outside. Grouped around the cloister are the refectory, chapter house, functional rooms and a skeletal remnant of the church.

St-Brieuc and the Côte de Goëlo listings

For Sleeping and Eating price codes and other relevant information, see page 13.

🛏 Where to stay

St-Brieuc *p64*

€€ Hôtel de Clisson, *36-38 rue de Gouët, T02 96 62 19 29, hoteldeclisson.com*. This hotel is well situated in the old centre near the cathedral. There are different categories of rooms – it's a good choice for single travellers – but all are comfortable and good value. Ask for one overlooking the pretty garden, where you can have breakfast in good weather. No restaurant, but a bar for guests' use only. There are also some private parking spaces, which is very useful in St-Brieuc.

€€-€ Hôtel Ker Izel, *20 rue de Gouët, T02 96 33 46 29, hotel-kerizel.com*. A well-priced hotel in an old house near the cathedral, with garden terrace and heated outdoor pool (summer only). Rooms are on the small size – in No 4 you might have to choose which bit of your body to put in the bathroom at one time – but they're comfortable enough and suitably equipped. A few car parking spaces are available in a garage along the street.

Côte de Goëlo *p65*

€€-€ Hôtel des Agapanthes, *1 rue Adrien Rebours, Ploubazlanec, T02 96 55 89 06, hotel-les-agapanthes.com*. Well situated near the coast between Paimpol and the ferry to Bréhat, this smart, comfortable hotel has pleasant rooms (some small) in two buildings, some with sea views and little terraces or balconies. Everything here is beautifully presented – reception, bedrooms, even the lavish breakfast buffet – in a modern chic style, with lots of attention to detail.

Chambres d'hôtes/gîtes

€€ Char à Bancs Ferme-Auberge, *Plélo,*

T02 96 79 51 25, aucharabanc.com. This is a really special place to stay, in a fantastic setting. There's a restaurant (in which they make their own cider) and a boating area in the bottom of the Leff valley. The delightful *gîtes/chambres d'hôtes* rooms are up a pretty track. The decor is sophisticated rural-chic, a fascinating blend of ancient and ultra modern, in a series of delightful little cottages. Gîtes cost up to €650 a week. A highly recommended choice.

€€ La Maison du Phare, *93 rue de la Tour, Plérin, T02 96 33 34 65, maisonphare.com*. A stylish green-shuttered, half-timbered B&B in a former merchant's house just past the port. Excellent designer-styled rooms, some with balcony/terrace, and one on the ground floor. Good sea views and well-placed for St-Brieuc centre or the coastal resorts, with easy parking and a bus route passing the door.

€€-€ Le Palus, *Plage du Palus, Plouha, T02 96 70 38 26, lepalus.fr*. The *chambres d'hôtes* option is a recent venture for this long-established restaurant (see Restaurants, below). It has a superb location right by the lovely beach Palus Plage, with sand-castling, swimming and a coastal path on its doorstep. The bright and simply furnished rooms are above the bar area, with sea or beach and cliff views. Good-value double or family rooms, and buffet breakfast.

🍴 Restaurants

St-Brieuc *p64*

€€ L'Air du Temps, *4 rue de Gouët, T02 96 68 58 40, airdutemps.fr. Tue-Sat 1200-1400, 1900-2130*. There's funky chic-trad decor in this restaurant, which is in an old house with a huge fireplace and beams. Specialities are fish and meat dishes *en cocotte* (casserole), with imaginative starters such as goat's cheese and Serrano ham with rhubarb compote. Vegetarian dishes if required. A three-course dinner with limited choice is under €20.

€€ Aux Pesked, *59 rue du Légué, T02 96 33 34 65, auxpesked.com. Tue-Fri 1200-1400, 1900-2300, Sat 1900-2300, Sun 1200-1400.* On the way to the Port de Légué, complete with large fish sculpture outside. A true gastronomic delight for fish-fanciers, now with a well-deserved Michelin star, from a *menu du pêcheur,* depending on the catch of the day, to the superlative chef's *menu de dégustation* at €85. Two- or three-course lunches for under €30 is a good-value treat.

€€-€ La Cuisine du Marché, *4/6 rue des Trois Frères Merlin, T02 96 61 70 94, lacuisinedumarche.net. Open 1200-1400, 1900-2200, closed Sun evening and Mon.* There's a good atmosphere in this bright, busy restaurant, equally popular with locals and visitors. There's lots of choice on the menu, with daily blackboard specials. The Breton sausage with light mustard sauce and creamy mashed potatoes is recommended, as is the café gourmand – a terrific selection of desserts plus strong coffee.

Côte de Goëlo *p65*

€€-€ La Ferme de Kerroc'h, *Route de Bréhat, Ploubazlanec, T02 96 55 81 75. Apr-Oct Wed-Sun and daily Jul and Aug 1200-1400, 1900-2130.* On the main road to the Bréhat ferry, this grill/crêperie offers a high standard of country cooking in a gorgeous old house with very fine stone doorways. Simple dishes – such as chicken in white wine sauce with rice – are full of flavour and attractively presented. Recommended.

€€-€ Le Palus/Restaurant La Homardine, *Palus Plage, Plouha, T02 96 70 38 26, lepalus. fr. Daily Apr-Oct, closed Tue in winter.* A varied choice with a brasserie/crêperie and a restaurant in this large establishment with upper and lower dining rooms, both overlooking the beach and sea. Seafood – *moules de bouchot à la crème,* oysters, langoustines – is the speciality, but there are steaks and crêpes too. Set menus from €20-30.

€ Fleur de Blé Noir Crêperie, *9 rue du Commandant, Malbert, St-Quay Portrieux, T02 96 70 31 55, fleurdeblenoir.com. Open 1200-1400, 1900-2200, closed Wed, Thu lunch and Sun dinner out of season, also closed Nov and Dec.* Opposite the casino and beach, this little crêperie has an upper room with some good sea views and an outdoor terrace. They serve very tasty savoury and sweet crêpes made with quality products. Give La Bisquine a try if you like caramel sauce and ice cream. The service is very friendly and there's a pleasant atmosphere.

🎭 Entertainment

St-Brieuc *p64*
Each Thursday and Friday evening in July and August, **Les Nocturnes** bring music and theatre to the streets. From punk and garage to clowns and puppets, there's something for every taste and age.

🛍 Shopping

St-Brieuc *p64*
Patisserie du Theatre, *3 rue Michelet, T02 96 33 41 68. 0845-1915, closed Mon and Sun afternoon.* Tiny shop with delicious cakes and coffee, also chocolate and sweets that would be suitable for presents, attractively gift-wrapped if required.

Terre de Terroirs, *5 rue St-Gilles, T02 96 33 02 01. Tue-Fri 0900-1300, 1530-1900, Sat 0800-1300, 1500-1900, Sun 1000-1200.* Delicatessen of minimalist decor selling superb regional products such as cheeses, cold meat, *foie gras* and smoked salmon, for a superior picnic.

🏔 What to do

Côte de Goëlo *p65*
Boat trips
Vedettes de Bréhat, *T02 96 55 79 50, vedettesdebrehat.com.* Ferries to the Ile de Bréhat from the Pointe de l'Arcouest, a trip of 10 minutes (return journey, adults

€9, children over four €7,50). On certain days they also offer four-hour sailings up the Trieux estuary, with a long stop at the Château de Roch Jagu (€21/15). Booking is advised in summer.

Train trips
La Vapeur du Trieux, *Av Général de Gaulle, Paimpol, T08 92 39 14 27, vapeurdutrieux.com*. This steam train runs along the Trieux valley between Pontrieux and Paimpol, stopping at the Maison de Traou-Nez, once the centre of a famous mystery murder. Sample local products served by costumed waitresses and listen to Breton musicians. Return trip, adults €23, children €11.50. Advance booking is recommended.

⊖ Transport

St-Brieuc *p64*
St-Brieuc centre is small enough to explore on foot. Buses do cover the Côte de Goëlo route, but less frequently outside summer. For times, see tibus.fr. A car is needed for sight-hopping.

Bus
The Gare Urbaine is in Boulevard Clemenceau (tubinfo.fr). Tickets €1,20 or 10 for €10,50. A three-hour ticket for combined town and district buses is €2.

Train
St-Brieuc station (Paris–Brest route) is at Place F Mitterand. Guingamp and Lannion also have train links.

❶ Directory

St-Brieuc *p64*
Banks ATMs on 3 rue de Rohan. **Medical services** Hospital and pharmacy 10 rue Marcel Proust, T02 96 01 71 23. **Post office** Place de la Résistance. **Tourist information** 7 rue St-Gouéno, T08 25 00 22 22, baiedesaintbrieuc.com, Monday-Saturday 0930-1230, 1330-1800, July and August 0930-1900, Sunday 1000-1300. Côtes d'Armor region: cotesarmor.com.

The Trégor

The world-renowned Pink Granite Coast is rightfully the jewel in the crown of this northwest area of Côtes d'Armor, but the sheer range of experiences on offer here, from megaliths to hi-tech exhibitions, is another powerful attraction. The busy coast around Perros-Guirec is balanced by the quieter green heart of the interior with its fine castles and handsome villages of warm yellow stone. The two main towns – bustling Lannion and dignified Tréguier – provide yet another contrast of pace and atmosphere.

Lannion → *For listings, see pages 76-78.*

Lannion is a busy and prosperous place, its success based on the telecommunications industry, with the research and development centre CNET based here since the 1960s. All that remains of the medieval château are a few glimpses of old ramparts, but many ancient houses still line the streets and flowery squares. The town flourished as a port in the 18th and 19th century, and the river Léguer is part of the centre's attraction. The friendly **tourist office** ① *T02 96 05 60 70, ot-lannion.fr, Jul-Aug 0900-1900, Sun 1000-1300, Sep-Jun 0930-1230, 1400-1800*, is on the Quai d'Aiguillon.

The Quays
Visiting the town to take the waters as a cure, the Duc d'Aiguillon, Commander-in-Chief of Brittany, saw the commercial potential of developing an inland port on the Léguer. He laid the first stone of the quays in 1762. The impressive building dominating the left bank of the river is the former Monastery of Ste-Anne, which now houses a *médiathèque* alongside the chapel. The adjoining park makes a good picnic spot by the river.

Place du Général Leclerc
Some very modern shopfronts and signs on one side of this square don't spoil the medieval feel of the other. Among these half-timbered houses from the 15th and 16th centuries, which once belonged to rich merchants, note the incredibly narrow Café Lannionais at No 31. Just to the east of the square, the Rue Cie Roger de Barbe also contains a row of ancient dwellings, and on the corner a plaque commemorates the Chevalier de Pont-Blanc, who fought heroically against the English here during the Wars of Succession.

Eglise de Brélévenez
A mini-pilgrimage up 140 steps leads to the lofty church of Brélévenez, which in part dates back to the 12th century. The church was possibly a foundation of the Knights Templar in the days of the crusades.

The oldest sculpture is the little group of the Ascension scene above the door of the sacristy. In the crypt, accessed by very narrow steps, is a graphic Entombment scene with life-size figures. Note also the holy-water stoop in the south aisle, which began life as a market measure for a bushel of wheat.

Around Lannion → *For listings, see pages 76-78.*

Le Yaudet
① *5 km west of Lannion.*
This delightful little hamlet on a natural defensive spur overlooking the entrance to the Léguer estuary is an important archaeological site, with excavations revealing Iron Age and Roman fortifications. A marked discovery path leads to impressive rock forms, coastguards' huts and an isolated *fontaine*, with constant flashes of view over the bay. (An informative leaflet is available from the Mairie in nearby Ploulec'h.) Don't miss the *Eglise Notre-Dame de Yaudet* and its intriguing oddity of a main altarpiece showing the Virgin lying in bed – literally – with the baby after the birth of Jesus. This is the perfect spot for a scenic picnic and an up-and-down walk, with steps leading to the water's edge. Or try the unpretentious *restaurant de terroir*, *Ar Vro* (see Restaurants, page 77).

Pleumeur-Bodou

ⓘ *7 km northwest of Lannion.*

Cité de Télécommunications ⓘ T02 96 46 63 80, cite-telecoms.com, Apr-Sep and school holidays 1000-1800, Sat and Sun 1400-1800, €7, €19.60 family. This large site is devoted to describing how telecommunications have developed over the decades. The father-founders Morse and Marconi have their place here, together with exhibits of equipment and interactive exercises. You can also speculate about the future: for example, will cars drive themselves in 20 years' time? Inside the adjoining Radôme is the antenna built in 1961-1962 to receive the first live television pictures from America via Telstar. It's a good place for young people, but if you tire of telecommunications, an excellent Planetarium (planetarium-bretagne.fr) and a Gaulish village (levillagegaulois.org) reconstruction for Asterix fans are nearby.

Menhir de St-Uzec This giant standing-stone is one of the best examples in Brittany of a Christianized menhir. The stone dates from Neolithic times but was elaborately engraved with symbols of Christ's passion in the 17th century, following the missions of Père Maunoir to root out paganism.

Château de Tonquédec

ⓘ *11 km south of Lannion, Tonquédec, T02 96 54 60 70, chateau-tonquedec.com. Apr, early Jun, late Sep 1400-1800, midJun-mid Sep 1000-1900, Oct Sat and Sun 1400-1730. €5/2.50.*
This is an impressive location for this fascinating château, situated on a spur overlooking the Léguer river. With drawbridges, turret stairs and dank cellars, it has all those elements essential to make a castle visit fun for all ages. Earliest parts date back to the 13th century, but most was rebuilt after being partly destroyed for supporting Charles de Blois in the Wars of Succession. The castle is now the property of the Le Rougé family, who are related to its original owners. As it's in private hands, the structure is less manicured than many, which adds to the sense of authenticity when scrambling about amid long grass and piles of rubble. Tonquédec was essentially a fortress rather than a home but domestic details remain in the tracery of chapel windows, fireplaces in former tower rooms and some fine latrines. You can also have a competition to see who can spot the most masons' marks on the stonework.

Perros-Guirec

ⓘ *9.5 km north of Lannion.*
Perros-Guirec is an attractive resort town, with all the traditional seaside attractions. The **Centre Ville** is on the hill-top above the two main beaches and busy pleasure port. The Port Miniature is a boating lake for family fun, and nearby there is a local museum (open Apr-May, Sep 0930-1215, 1400-1800, Jun-Aug 0930-1830, €3/€1.50) with a collection of *coiffes* (lace headdresses) and exhibitions of Breton history, including the Atlantic Wall defences used in this area in the Second World War. The casino provides more active entertainment or, as a contrast, try the thalassotherapy centre for the languid sensations of a salt-water spa. From the Gare Maritime near the Plage de Trestaou, you can take a boat to the Sept-Iles or reach the starting point for a walk along the famous Pink Granite Coast.

Tréguier

ⓘ *20 km east of Lannion.*
Tréguier is a most appealing town, with its glorious cathedral, half-timbered houses, cafés, restaurants and waterside spaces. The tourist office is situated in a tower building by the

River Jaudy, the port area in the commercial heyday. The old houses in the town reflect this same 16th-century prosperity, mostly based on the cloth trade. A large Neolithic reconstruction sits on the river bank unobtrusively, by the easiest parking area. Stroll up the colourful Rue Renan, which honours the writer and philosopher Ernest Renan, whose work, such as *Life of Jesus*, often challenged the accepted tenets of Catholicism. His statue keeps an ironic eye on the cathedral and the house where he was born in 1823 contains a museum dedicated to the great man.

Around the Place du Martray are many twisty streets with a vibrant variety of architectural detail from different periods. The Rue Colvestre has half-timbered houses of the 16th century and the earlier Maison du Duc Jean V, which now contains a bookshop. Further up, only the Flamboyant-Gothic doorway remains of the Vieil Evêché, built in 1430.

In Place du Général Leclerc is a memorial to 500 years of printing in Tréguier, which saw Jehan Calvez produce the first French/Latin/Breton dictionary in 1499. Off the Boulevard Anatole Le Braz ahead, the Bois du Poète is an appealingly unkempt park beside the river. It contains a simple stele to Anatole Le Braz, one of the most famous native writers, whose collections of oral testimony have done so much to preserve Breton traditions.

Cathédrale St-Tugdual This magnificent structure is on the spot of the foundation of Welsh monk St-Tugdual, one of the founding saints of Brittany, but today it is the home of St-Yves.

Yves Hélory was born near here in 1253 and became a lawyer renowned for his impartiality between rich and poor, a rare thing in medieval times. He was canonised in 1347 and became the patron saint of Brittany, celebrated today in an extremely well-attended Pardon on the third Sunday in May.

Largely a fine Gothic remodelling, the north transept of the cathedral retains hints of the earlier Romanesque architecture. At the Revolution it was sacked by soldiers, so the impressive tomb of St-Yves, originally ordered by Duke Jean V, is an identical copy. The precious relic of his skull is also proudly on display. In a side-chapel is the tomb of the duke himself, whose long reign (1399-1442) brought a period of stability after the Wars of Succession. The greyhound symbolizing Brittany lies at his feet.

Don't miss the cloister here, for its own sake and for the best views of the two towers and later spire.

Pink Granite Coast

Perros-Guirec is the best starting point to admire the wonders of the Pink Granite Coast, following Le Sentier des Douaniers, the Customs' Officers Path, along the coast to Ploumanac'h, a distance of about 3 km. Prepare for some awesome and amusing sights among the extraordinary variety of shapes and textures on view. Granite is a volcanic rock in origin, pushed up from the centre of the earth to the surface by the expanding heat of magma, then cooling and falling prey to erosion over millions of years. The granite here is a mixture of black mica, greyish quartz and rose-coloured feldspar; its pink tinge becomes more pronounced in certain lights. The rocks along this stretch of coastline have been transformed by the power of the tides and winds into all manner of fantastic shapes. The outer sections crumbled away into sand, leaving hard cores to tumble and settle into the kaleidoscope of forms now on show. Many have been given names, like The Tortoise, Death's Head and Napoleon's Hat – there is certainly plenty of scope for using your imagination to the full.

Access to the path begins above the Plage de Trestraou behind the Gare Maritime. The islands visible offshore are the Sept-Îles, an important nature reserve with thousands of seabirds. The way is fairly level and easygoing and after 800 m you can see large formations looming ahead. The first elaborate conglomeration is known as the Devil's Castle, for obvious reasons. Round the point of the Skevell, the path passes a little Custom Officers' lookout (*guérite*) used for watching for smugglers, and a powder store close by, before reaching the cove of Pors Kamor. This is the remnant of an ancient river valley, a scenic spot today where the light-blue water contrasts strikingly with the glow of the rocks. Continue past the lifeboat station and lighthouse, and you soon reach the **Maison du Littoral** ① *summer Mon-Sat 1000-1300, 1400-1800, school holidays Mon-Fri 1400-1700, Wed 1400-1700 all year*, which has displays about nature and geology in this unique environment.

Rounding the next point to the Plage St-Guirec brings yet another wonder with this bay, a rock-strewn jumble at low tide. This is the beach where Saint Guirec landed in Brittany in the sixth century, according to legend, in a stone boat. Just by the stone cross in the corner is a plaque commemorating the code message 'Is Napoleon's hat still at Perros-Guirec?' transmitted to the Breton resistance by the BBC from London in 1944.

The prominent island château of Costaérès at the mouth of the bay dates from the 1890s. Here Polish author Henri Sienkiewicz finished writing his famous novel *Quo Vadis*. On the beach is the raised oratory of Saint Guirec, lapped by waves at high tide. Legend has it that sticking a pin in the saint's nose would ensure marriage within a year. This is why the granite statue here now was needed to replace an earlier wooden one that lost its nose from repeated assaults. But even granite can't stand up against determination, as you can see.

The rocky spectacle comes to an end as you continue up past the nearby chapel and round the rocks to come out at the port of Ploumanac'h, where a dam with tide-mill crosses the estuary. You can either retrace your steps or take a detour through the Vallée des Traïouero inland. The name actually means the 'Valley of the Valleys' thanks to a French cartographer's misunderstanding of Breton in the 18th century. It can feel like a lost world to explore the many paths, caves and wild vegetation around the lake and feeder streams. This place provides a welcome, shady refuge from the coast on a hot day, and the greenery can come as a relief after all those gleaming rocks.

The Trégor listings

For Sleeping and Eating price codes and other relevant information, see page 13.

⊙ Where to stay

The Trégor *p71*

€€€-€€ Hôtel Aigue Marine, *Port de Plaissance, Tréguier, T02 96 92 97 00, aiguemarine-hotel.com.* Situated on the waterfront, a short uphill walk to the town centre, this bright, comfortable hotel has large, well-equipped rooms with balconies overlooking the river. Very friendly service, and a modern restaurant where chef Yoann Peron's fish dishes are reliably excellent. The breakfast buffet is a treat in itself. The hotel also has a garden with an outdoor swimming pool, and gym/sauna.

€€€ Manoir du Sphinx, *Chemin de la Messe, Perros- Guirec, T02 96 23 25 42, lemanoirdusphinx.com.* An attractive cliff-top villa, well placed for the facilities of the town, yet in a peaceful spot. It also offers superb views over the Sept-Iles. Rooms are comfortable and well equipped, and some have full-glass bay windows to make the most of the location. Try some gourmet seafood in the chandeliered dining room.

€€ Ar Vro, *Le Yaudet, T02 96 46 48 80, restaurant-pension-ar-vro.com.* Spend a night in this tranquil and beautiful village near Lannion and the coast. Of the five pleasant rooms at Ar Vro, one has a view over the bay. A stay here on the basis of demi-pension, enables you to take advantage of the excellent restaurant where *produits du terroir* (see Eating, page 77). About €60 per person (based on two sharing) including bed, breakfast and dinner, is good value.

€€ Villa Cyrnos, *10 rue du Sergent l'Héveder, Perros-Guirec, T02 96 91 13 36, villacyrnos22. monsite-orange.fr.* On the way down to the port, this large house in well-kept gardens has five bedrooms, including two adjoining, suitable for families. Old family photos create a homely feel, and Roger Guyon is an obliging host. Ask for a room with a sea view; if there isn't one available, at the very least you can enjoy a panoramic perspective from the breakfast room.

€ Chambres d'hôtes de Scavet, *10 rue Ker Coz, Tréguier, T02 96 92 94 18, chambresdescavet.fr.* This house of pink granite is very conveniently placed near the cathedral. It offers two good-sized bedrooms, each en suite, separated by a large kitchen/dining/sitting area where guests can prepare their own meals. This communal space is pleasant and eclectically decorated, giving the feel of staying in a friend's house. Gaëlle Huon-Tregros serves delicious breads and home-made jam for breakfast.

€€ Kerlilou, *3 Calvary, Plouguiel, T02 96 92 24 06, kerlilou.fr.* Well located for town and coast, this is a lovely old house with garden setting, a positive haven for those seeking quality accommodation in a tranquil location. The large, beautifully decorated rooms with period furniture also have spacious bathrooms, hot drinks trays and internet access. The welcoming hosts can provide dinner every night except Sunday. A useful stop for walkers, as the GR34 coastal path passes the property.

€ Tara B&B, *31 rue Ernest Renan, Tréguier, T02 96 92 15 28, chambrestaratreguier.com.* An almost secret location in an ancient house behind the owner's shop, yet right in the centre of town. There are five en suite rooms (one suitable for the disabled), each with its own Irish title. The name Tara (home of the early kings of Ireland) reflects Guy Arhant's ancestry: he and his wife Malou, who speak English, happily share their enthusiasm for Celtic traditions in a real Breton home. A corner kitchen is available for guests to prepare their own evening meals, which can then be enjoyed outside in the enticing gardens.

Gîtes

Gîtes-en-Trégor, *Guergillès Guirec, Ploubezre, T02 96 47 17 86, gites-en-tregor.*

com. Three lovely gîtes in a quiet location near the Chapelle de Kerfons, well placed for visiting the Trégor. Clara and Martin Cronin are helpful on-site hosts, and can advise on walking (the GR34A is nearby) and sightseeing. Families are welcome, with the possibility of using two adjoining houses for larger groups. Le Grange is suitable for disabled visitors. Smaller gîtes (sleeping four) from €325, larger (for eight) from €725.

Camping

Camping de Traou-Mélédern, *Pontrieux, T02 96 95 69 27, campingpontrieux.free.fr.* An excellent position for this quiet site by the Trieux river, with spacious pitches for tents and caravans, and accommodation to rent. Regulars of many nationalities appreciate the helpful owners and clean facilities. You can rent a gîte (two or five person) or mobile home from €260-380 a week. Camping for two people is about €15 per night. Open all year.

🍴 Restaurants

The Trégor *p71*

€€ Ar Vro, *Le Yaudet, T02 96 46 48 80, restaurant-ar-vro.com. Every day Jul and Aug (not Mon lunch) closed Mon and Tue out of season, 1230-1330 and 1930-2045.* This restaurant with rooms has a reputation for chef André Minne's fine cooking. The emphasis is on local products of quality, with fish figuring strongly on the menu. The €26 *menu du terroir* might include a starter of *foie gras* presented in the form of a crème brûlée. Filet of monkfish with fennel and creamed quinoa is recommended.

€€-€ Auberge du Trégor, *3 rue St-Yves, Tréguier, T02 96 92 32 34, aubergedutregor. com. Tue-Sat 1200-1400, 1900-2100, Sun 1200-1330.* Near the cathedral, this beautiful old stone house has a pretty dining room. Christian Turpault works wonders in the kitchen, while his wife welcomes diners with good-value set menus and a tempting *carte*. Goat's cheese with bacon and apples,

followed by scallops and prawn with artichokes in a vanilla sauce might leave room for an apricot version of Breton *far*.

€ Le Moulin Vert, *15 rue Duguesclin, Lannion, T02 96 37 91 20, creperielemoulinvert. com. Daily 1200-1400 and from 1830.* You can't miss the green windmill signs outside this attractively decorated corner restaurant. Menus decorated with local scenes, bright tablecloths and plants all contribute to a pleasant atmosphere. The simple food is excellent, focusing on salads, *galettes* or pasta dishes – try a warm salad with Breton sausage. Very popular with both locals and tourists.

Cafés and bars

Le Lannionais, *31 place du Général Leclerc, Lannion.* Squeeze into the very welcoming atmosphere of this ancient half-timbered building. The small bar area inside has a superb beamed ceiling, but it's nicer to sit outside and enjoy the bustle of the main square.

Le Manoir Elfique (Manoir de Kerloas), *Plouléc'h, signed off the main Lannion/ Morlaix road, T02 96 46 36 64, taverne-elfira. fr., Mon, Wed-Fri 1700-0100, Sat and Sun 1130-1400, 1700-0100.* A cultural venture in a fine 15th-century château, with a café/ bar offering food ranging from tapas to boeuf bourguinon. The events programme includes exhibitions, concerts and storytellers.

🛍 Shopping

The Trégor *p71*
Clothing

La Goélette, *135 rue de Saint-Guirec, Ploumanac'h, T02 96 91 40 90. Feb to mid-Nov daily 0930-1930 (except Sat and Sun morning).* A treasure trove of marine fashion Breton-style, this store is packed with all the well-known makes, such as Le Glazik and Armor-Lux, for men, women and children.

Food and drink

Au Fournil Gourmand, *16 place du Général Leclerc, Lannion. Tues-Sat 0730-1930, Sun 0730-1300.* Despite changing from its famous wood-fired oven to gas for baking, the quality here is still excellent. Pizzas and fruit tarts are delicious, or try their Flûte Gana speciality bread.

▲ What to do

The Trégor *p71*
Boat trips

Vedettes de Perros-Guirec, *Gare Maritime, T02 96 91 10 00, armor-decouverte.fr.* A boat trip around the Sept-Iles is a must for bird lovers. Various options are available – a two-hour trip including the islands and Pink Granite Coast is €17.50 for an adult, €11.50 for children. Some trips make a short landing on the Ile aux Moines.

Flights

Aéro-Club de la Côte de Granite, *T02 96 48 47 42, accg.asso.fr.* From Lannion, you can take a flight over the Pink Granite Coast lasting 15 minutes (€70 for two people), or go further afield to the Côtes des Ajoncs or above the Manoirs of the Léguer valley, with 30 minutes at €120.

Waterparks

Armoripark, *Bégard, T02 96 45 36 36, armoripark.com. Apr-Sep, 1100-1800 (1900 in summer). €11/€10 high season.* Children will love a visit to this aquatic park, where there are many fun pools, bumper boats, trampolines, playgrounds (including one for toddlers only) and farm animals.

Contents

Background

History

Celts and Romans

From around 750 BC peoples from the east of Europe and the Black Sea area gradually infiltrated northwest France. These are often referred to collectively as Celts, although their connections were probably cultural rather than racial. How many of them actually reached Brittany is debatable, but their cultural influences certainly permeated the peninsula, which embraced five tribes – the Osismes, Vénètes, Coriosolites, Riedones and Namnètes. Brittany was Armor, land of the sea. Finds of coin hoards and jewellery indicate the fine quality of their metalworking, and they had many trading links with Cornwall and the rest of Britain. Their polytheistic religion, reverence for nature and priestly class of Druids left a legacy that survived through the centuries. Their main structural survivals are the many Iron Age fortified peninsulas to be seen around the west coast of Brittany.

Despite a propensity for tribal warfare, the Celts were ultimately no match for Roman military organization. Julius Caesar had a fleet built to challenge the most powerful tribe – the Vénètes – at sea in the Gulf of Morbihan, and after his victory the Roman province of Armorica was established. It is doubtful if many Romans settled here, but the benefits of Roman civilization were certainly felt by the wealthier strata of the tribes who would have provided the local officials and built villas in the Roman style. A well-preserved bath complex at Hogolo on the coast in Côtes d'Armor reflects a new standard of living for some.

Remaining evidence of Roman occupation is not as widespread as one might expect, but there are some exceptional sites such as Corseul, with its octagonal Temple of Mars, and a fish-processing factory at Douarnenez in Finistere.

The age of saints

The story of Brittany really begins in the fifth and sixth centuries with the influx of migrants from Great Britain in the aftermath of Roman imperialism and the solid spread of Anglo-Saxon culture across England. Contacts between the two countries had been established for thousands of years – the journey was only a day's sail in good conditions and similarities of language indicate close communication. In fact the fusion of indigenous dialects with the speech of the incomers is the origin of the Breton language. The name Brittany means Little Britain.

The territory at this time was divided into a series of small kingdoms. According to legend this was the Age of Saints, when Celtic monks and their followers primarily from Ireland and Wales crossed the channel to settle and build religious foundations. Stories of arrivals in stone boats probably reflect a scribal linguistic confusion of the Latin *cumba* (small boat) and old Breton *koum* (valley or hollowed-out stone trough). Generally the newcomers appear to have been well received, but the mixture of history and legend characteristic of this period is well illustrated by tales retaining hints of some localized opposition. Tales tell of saints such as Ronan and Ké being attacked and vilified on arrival.

There was a marked difference between the east and west of Brittany – the terms Haute and Basse Bretagne being used in the sense of nearer and further. Nearer, of course, meant nearer to seats of power elsewhere, whether Rome or Paris, as the empire of the Franks began to expand all over France. After the conversion of Clovis in AD 496, this meant the official Christianity of the Roman church. The east of Brittany developed under the

Megaliths

Brittany has some of the most important Neolithic sites in Europe, including the alignments at Carnac and the tallest standing stone (nearly 11 m) in France in northwest Finistère (page 000). Burial sites from as early as 6000 BC are numerous enough to suggest a sizeable early population in the peninsula. And from an even earlier time, long before the channel separated Great Britain from the continent, there is evidence of habitation and the use of fire at Menez Dregan, with a date around 450,000 BC.

The main characteristics of the New Stone Age (c 5000-2000 BC) are that man began to settle on the land, clear forests, grow crops, tend animals, make pottery and weave fabric. Although these people have not left us any domestic buildings in Brittany, their monuments in stone show a remarkable mastery of construction and a high degree of social organization. We do not know exactly what their intentions were or what practical use the structures had, but group celebrations on a large scale were clearly the purpose of alignments such as those at Carnac and St-Just. Here, there are long rows of raised stones and burial places over a wide area, so the sites must have been a focal point for worship, community activities and the cult of the dead for many centuries. Elsewhere menhir ('long stones' in Breton) often appear to stand alone in the countryside, but so many have been lost that these may well have been part of related chains stretching for very long distances. They probably served as boundaries, directional markers or indicators of sacred burial sites. There are many forms of burial chambers to be seen in Brittany, most commonly dolmen (stone tables) or elongated *allées couvertes* (covered passages). These were often reused over hundreds of years, so objects excavated in them may date from different periods. The use of metals came with Bronze Age developments, when burial mounds tended to be more singular, suggesting a more hierarchical society, with important leaders receiving special round tombs.

influence of the Romans and then the Franks, with the resultant use of Latin and Gallo, a language derived from Latin. The Church of Rome held sway here with bishops of Breton sees appointed by the Pope under the authority of the Metropolitan bishop of Tours. In the west, matters were very different. The new religious leaders were simple holy men, sometimes hermits rather than worldly officials. They lived among their people and in nature, until drawn into political life by kings, such as Gradlon of Quimper, who persuaded St-Corentin to give up his rural life and become bishop of a new cathedral. If there were attempts to stamp out paganism (as tales of saints exorcizing the land of fierce dragons tend to suggest), then total success appears to have eluded the early Christians, given the mass of 'pagan' detail in decorative religious sculpture right up to the 17th century.

The emergence of Brittany

As the Franks began to expand their control throughout what is modern France, and powerful emperors such as Pepin the Short and Charlemagne sought domination, conflict with Brittany was inevitable. What is now eastern Brittany, roughly the department of Ille-et-Vilaine, became a sort of buffer zone, with Frankish lords installed to defend or attack as required. In the early ninth century, Louis the Pious made forays into Brittany against war-like leaders such as Morvan, whose territory was around Langonnet but, while the army of the Franks could use sheer weight of numbers to overcome the Bretons in open fighting, they could not triumph against the sort of guerrilla tactics employed in the undulating hills and sinuous valleys of the interior. Each time authority seemed to have been imposed and Louis focused his attention elsewhere, there was trouble. Eventually he tried another tack and appointed a Breton, Nominoë, as Count of Vannes and *missus imperatoris*, the Emperor's representative. Peace was maintained in this way for Louis' lifetime, but when Charles the Bald took over, he was soon at loggerheads with Nominoë, who led Breton raids into the border lands. At the battle of Ballon (Bains-sur-Oust) in AD 845 the Bretons scored a stunning victory and Charles had no choice but to come to terms. Nominoë's son Erispoë kept up the same momentum and Charles had to grant him the title king and give up the lands of Rennes and Nantes. This period saw the naissance of a Breton state.

The Viking menace soon distracted both Bretons and Franks from their hostilities. Towns, villages, abbeys and islands were raided, with much destruction of resources, and more significantly, an exodus of nobles to France. Their later return brought French language and political influences to the detriment of Breton development.

A telling victory over the Vikings by Alain the Great at Questembert in AD 888 brought a temporary lull, but the horror was not over. After Landévennec Abbey was sacked in AD 913, the abbot called on another Alain, grandson of the first, who had been brought up at the court of Athelstan in England. Alain Barbetorte, as he became known, finally managed to put an end to the Viking threat in Brittany and made Nantes the new capital of his dukedom.

Normans and Plantagenets

Feuding rivals after his death brought more outside interference in Brittany, as William of Normandy battled around Dinan in support of a contender to the dukedom. Later, many Bretons were to cross the channel with him on the 1066 invasion of England, and subsequently held lands there in reward for their prowess.

The Plantagenets were next to try for control in Brittany, with Henry II using Conan IV, a weak duke, to rule indirectly before coming in person to besiege nobles opposed to his puppet. He finally arranged for his son Geoffrey to marry Conan's daughter and become duke in 1175. After Henry's death, French King Philippe Auguste, supported Arthur, Geoffrey's son, against the English King John. John had Arthur murdered, but Pierre de Dreux, cousin of the French king, married Alix, Arthur's half-sister, and became duke.

So in 1213, Brittany was already inextricably linked to France. The supremacy of the duke did not go unchallenged, and the lords of Léon and Penthièvre constantly strived to retain autonomy and fortify their territories. The successors of Pierre de Dreux brought a degree of stability and prosperity to Brittany, but when Jean III died in 1341 without naming an heir, all hell broke loose.

Wars of Succession
There were two claimants to the duchy, both related to Jean III. Jean de Monfort was his half-brother, and Jeanne de Penthièvre his niece. She was married to Charles de Blois, nephew of the king of France, so French support was assured for their side. Most of the high nobility also supported them, while Jean de Montfort, on the other hand, could call on English troops thanks to his connections with Edward III, and on much of Basse Bretagne.

The armed conflict, part of the Hundred Years War, caused appalling damage and loss of life on Breton soil for more than 20 years. Jean de Montfort was tricked into custody in Paris, then freed by the efforts of his wife after the Treaty of Malestroit in 1341. He died soon after his release, but the war continued and Charles de Blois was captured in 1347, then kept prisoner in England for years. The famous Battle of the Thirty took place in 1351 near Josselin, with Beaumanoir's Breton side victorious and 18 English captives later ransomed. Jean de Montfort's son took up his father's cause and a decisive battle was fought near Auray in 1364. Charles de Blois was killed and the king of France finally had to acknowledge Jean IV as duke of Brittany.

The struggle with France

A period of stability under the Montfort dynasty enabled trade to flourish, especially during the long rule of Jean V (1399-1442), despite a final Penthièvre flurry of revenge when they captured the duke and held him prisoner for four months. When he was freed, their estates were confiscated, but the continuing antagonism of certain noble families did much to undermine Brittany's independence and security.

Tensions with the French court came to a head in the time of Duke François II. Louis XI laid claim to Brittany, and François called on the Breton council Les Etats de Bretagne to ensure the rights of his two daughters, Anne and Isabeau. He hoped to marry Anne to the Austrian emperor Maximilian, to keep the French out, but many of the Breton nobility, looking to their own advancement, sided openly with France. Armed conflict ensued and the French were victorious in a decisive battle at St-Aubin-du-Cormier in 1488.

François died soon after and Anne, aged 11, became a political pawn. Her supporters engineered a marriage by proxy to Maximilian but Charles VIII, newly crowned king of France, marched into Brittany and forced an annulment before marrying Anne himself. To keep Brittany firmly in French control, a clause in their wedding contract said that in the event of his death, Anne must marry his successor. When Charles did die suddenly, Anne became the wife of the new king, Louis XII.

As Duchess of Brittany, Anne was a popular figure, later taken as a symbol of her region's independence from France, although the political reality was rather different. Patron of the arts and religiously devout, Anne toured her duchy to rapturous welcomes and lavish gifts. Her image today remains a powerful evocation of medieval Brittany at its height. But of her eight children, only two girls survived infancy and she feared for the future of Brittany. Rightly so – Anne died in 1514 and Louis a year later, but he insisted before his death on the marriage of their daughter Claude to François d'Angoulême, heir to the French throne. Claude could not be expected to resist the pressures of French dominance, and in 1532 an act of Union was signed at Vannes, making Brittany part of France. Important special privileges retained were exemption from military service outside Brittany, trials for Bretons before Breton courts, and no imposition of new taxes without the consent of the Etats. It was the end of an era, but the culmination of a long trend of Frenchification among the Breton upper classes.

Prosperity and war

A new period of peace and stability fostered Brittany's Golden Age of prosperity and artistic development. Towns and villages were permanent building sites as cathedrals, chapels and houses sprang up. The linen trade with England continued to flourish with

Morlaix, Guingamp and Quintin much occupied in its execution. Fishing was also a major prop of the economy with boats from St-Malo and the Côte de Goëlo making the long journey to Newfoundland for cod as early as the 1520s.

Brittany got a new Parliament body in 1552, as the main court of justice for the region. Rennes, now the capital, was the location, with a suitably fine building later erected to house it.

The Wars of Religion, which affected much of France, once again brought soldiers and destruction to Brittany. The Duke de Mercoeur, governor and fanatical Catholic, set up his power base around Nantes in defiance of the French king, Henri IV, and the proclamation of tolerance for Protestants. He was determined to stamp out Protestantism in the region. Although most of Brittany was Catholic in faith, some powerful noble families, like Lavals and Rohans, were Protestant and this had some effect through their wide land-holdings. Towns like Brest and Rennes remained loyal to the king, as did the Breton Parliament.

Between 1589 and 1598, war raged across the region. Foreign soldiers poured in, the English in favour of the Protestant cause and the Spanish to support the Catholics. The Pointe des Espagnols in the Crozon Peninsula is an echo of a fortress from this period. St-Malo declared its independence as a Republic, which lasted four years before they surrendered to the king. In 1593 Henri IV converted to Catholicism to put an end to the war. He came to Brittany and accepted the surrender of the Duke of Mercoeur. The Edict of Nantes (1598) granted freedom of worship to Protestants.

Revival

The post-war relief was deep, and new expressions of counter-reformation religious faith burst out in further construction of convents and chapels. In western Brittany the extraordinary parish closes, exquisitely decorated church precincts, came to life. There was also a revival of the missionary spirit, largely fuelled by Michel le Nobletz, born in Finistère in 1577. He travelled in western Brittany teaching and encouraging the poor to adhere to the Catholic faith. He used painted maps to represent biblical stories and parables (these *taolennou* were painted on wood or animal skins) in the same way that the stories of Jesus' passion on the calvaries were used to teach often illiterate parishioners. Père Julien Maunoir was le Nobletz's energetic successor, bringing thousands back into the fold but, coming from eastern Brittany, he did not speak Breton. A quick learner, he was soon able to continue the work, but the official story went that an angel had touched him on the lips and given him the gift of speaking Breton at once.

The early part of the 17th century saw a development of the ports and naval facilities of Brittany under the auspices of the new governor, Cardinal Richelieu. In 1631 Brest was designated as the main military port, to take advantage of its vast protected roadstead or Rade. Lorient was created in 1666 as a place of naval construction and a home for the trading organization *Compagnie des Indes*, and Nantes was an already an important international trading centre.

The beginning of the end

As early as 1632 there were signs of tension in the terms of the Union, as the *Etats* made formal complaints to Louis XIII about the amounts of money being demanded by the crown as 'gifts' in breach of the original agreement, whereby their assent was required. It was glossed over on this occasion but this was to become the recurrent theme of relations between France and Brittany.

The determination of Colbert, finance minister of Louis XIV, to wrest money through taxation drove the first nails into the coffin of Brittany's traditional economy. Taxes on tobacco and stamped paper for legal transactions were announced without the agreement of the *Etats*, which led to rioting in the streets of Rennes and Nantes. The unrest spread to rural areas, particularly in western Brittany with the revolt of the Bonnets Rouges in 1675. After negotiations with the English and Dutch, this uprising found itself leaderless when Sebastien Le Balp was murdered by an aristocratic prisoner.

The peasants of Pays Bigouden were determined to pursue their claims to justice and protection from the abuses of the nobility. Rallying to the summons of church bells, they seized the towns of Pont l'Abbé and Concarneau before the Duc de Chaulnes arrived to ruthlessly quash the rebellion. In Combrit where the local lord had been murdered, 14 peasants were hanged from the same tree in reprisal. The bell towers of churches at the heart of the rebellion were taken down as a symbolic punishment – the church of Lambour in Pont l'Abbé remains an evocative reminder today. Rennes was also penalized, with the Breton Parliament exiled to Vannes until 1690.

Signs of unrest

The 18th century saw increasing social and political tensions in Brittany. The growth of towns and mercantile trade brought divisions between urban and rural areas and priorities. The gulf between rich and poor was felt by the peasants struggling with burdens of cultivation, taxation and obligation. The development of a commercial class who had money but little power was also an issue simmering below the surface. Louis XIV died in 1715 but his successors continued to make demands as European conflicts increased military spending. English blockades of Breton ports and raids on the land were a constant actual and psychological battle.

During the Seven Years War (1756-1763) St-Malo was a target for English attacks. Failing there, they landed further west and were surrounded when attempting to re-embark at St-Cast, with more than 2000 casualties.

Nantes was now the second port in France and made much of its wealth from the slave-trade, with boats taking goods to Africa to exchange for slaves then moving on to the West Indies to exchange slaves for luxury goods like sugar to bring back to Nantes. Shipbuilding was also important there, and at Brest where the arsenal employed nearly 5000 people. Meanwhile Breton corsairs confronted France's commercial rivals, the English and Dutch, in the Channel and on the high seas worldwide.

An event of 1764 brought political tensions to crisis point. In the so-called Affaire de Bretagne, there was a clash between La Chalotais, president of the Breton parliament and the Duc d'Aiguillon, Commander-in-Chief of the region. Louis XV intervened to poor effect: when the Bretons refused to obey him, he resorted to the extreme of dissolving Parliament. La Chalotais was arrested and imprisoned, accused of political incitement, but his support held firm and eventually the new king, Louis XVI, freed him in 1774 and restored the rights of Parliament.

French Revolution
Initially the French Revolution was generally favoured in Brittany for obvious reasons. Many were tired of what they saw as the oppression and injustice of the nobility and no one was keen on the constant demands for money to fund French quarrels. The earliest clashes of the Revolution took place on the streets of Rennes, and Bretons were at the forefront of the revolt in Paris, through the influential Club Breton. Guy Le Guen de Kerangall from Landivisiau made an influential speech against the nobility in the French Assembly.

Early moves by the Revolutionary authorities in Paris to recognize regional differences by producing decrees in various languages, including Breton, were reassuring. The Breton representatives agreed to cede the special privileges Brittany had enjoyed since union in 1532 – what need was there in the new age of equality and republicanism? The Breton Parliament and the *Etats* were formally abolished in 1789. Brittany was divided into five departments – Côtes-du-Nord (now Côtes d'Armor), Finistère, Morbihan, Ille-et-Vilaine and Loire-Inférieure. As there was only to be one bishopric per department, four were lost at Dol-de-Bretagne, St-Pol, St-Malo and Tréguier.

It was largely the issue of religion that changed a swathe of public opinion in Brittany. In 1791 all clergy were pressured to swear an oath of allegiance to the Republic. Some 75% in Brittany - as many as 95% In parts of the west - refused and were ousted from their parishes. Many went into hiding and still gave secret mass for their loyal followers. When anti-clerical measures began to come into force, and peasants realized they were no better off than under their noble masters, many pockets of resistance to revolutionary ideas grew up. As early as 1791 the Marquis de la Rouërie had founded a Catholic, anti-revolutionary, pro-monarchy movement around Fougères. This soon fizzled out with his death, but the Chouan uprisings further south in the Vendée found an echo in certain parts of Brittany. Morbihan was a stronghold for Chouan bands, who mostly worked independently. One leader, Cadoudal, was part of a plan to land English forces at Quiberon to support the Chouans. This was a tragic failure as the attackers were hemmed in on the peninsula and then forced to surrender or were killed by General Hoche.

When Prussia and Austria began hostilities against France, Bretons were called up into the French army, as their old exemption was lost. Many young Bretons preferred to go into hiding or join Chouan bands rather than leave their homeland. In 1800, the bishop of Quimper, who had voted for the decapitation of Louis XVI, was murdered on the road by Chouan activists. When Napoleon came to power he sent troops to put an end to Chouannerie once and for all. Pontivy, the military centre in Morbihan where the counter-revolutionaries were most active, was renamed Napoleonville. Cadoudal was eventually arrested and executed in 1804. The Emperor took some steps to calm the situation. His Concordat with the Pope in 1801 allowed priests to return, and he gave a short exemption from service outside Brittany to those of military age.

Another consequence of European opposition to the Revolution was the construction of the Nantes–Brest canal. It was given the go-ahead by Napoleon as a strategic defensive measure for cross-Brittany transport at a time when the English were blockading Breton ports. It was to link the arsenals at Nantes, Brest and Hennebont (in conjunction with the Blavet canal) and provide a secure internal supply route. In fact the canal's main use on completion 30 years later was commercial rather than military.

Tough times

The first half of the 19th century was a challenging one in Brittany. No longer with special privileges, Bretons found their culture and language under threat in an era of conformity and uniformity. The Church, mainstay of Breton's strong social cohesion, faced hard challenges within a secular state. A decree of 1793 said that teaching should be in French only and, as much education in Brittany was delivered by Breton-speaking priests, it seemed to be an anti-clerical measure.

Political parties gradually emerged, with the Blues, who were republican, progressive and hostile to traditionalists and the Church, and the conservative

Whites, aristocrats and clergy who had the support of many dependent peasants. An exception was in the Monts d'Arrée, where some of the poorest people in Brittany took the side of progress. Area support for these groups pretty much mirrored current 21st-century voting, with Léon, Morbihan and eastern Ille-et-Vilaine essentially with the conservative Whites, and the rest of Finistère and the Trégor with the Blues.

Economic progress was mixed. Traditional industries such as the cloth trade and foundries were in decline and agriculture suffered from a lack of manpower as foreign wars continued to rage. Even in the 1840s people were dying of famine and pestilence, and rural life was grim. Inland ports such as Morlaix and Redon declined as ships got larger, while Lorient flourished.

Communications improved as the Nantes–Brest canal was finally finished in 1842 and the railway pushed its way into Brittany; by 1865 Quimper, Rennes and Brest were linked to the main French network, and numerous branch lines in the latter part of the century saw commercial and touristic development for places like Douarnenez, Roscoff and Dinard.

Agriculture began to expand with better fertilization available, and more land came under cultivation. But overall there was a decline in the numbers of the rural population as larger towns, like Rennes, grew. Towards the end of the century as many as 300,000 Bretons left Brittany for Paris, other large towns or abroad.

This period also saw a great revival of antiquarian interest in the 'Celtic' aspect of Breton development. The URB (Union Régionaliste Bretonne) was formed in 1898, to study Breton language, folklore and oral traditions.

Industrially, as factories grew so did disputes between bosses and workers. Unions began in the 1890s and strikes became common, often leading to violence. Politics saw the formation of the earliest Breton Nationalist Party (PNB) in 1911. Numerous Bretons lost their lives on the battlefields of the First World War, which also saw the arrival of many foreigners – workers, refugees, the wounded, American soldiers – in Brittany. The most elaborate Great War memorial in Brittany is at St-Anne d'Auray in Morbihan.

Moving towards modernity

Between the wars, Brittany had France's first communist mayor at Douarnenez in 1921, but political power swung between conservatives and socialists. The Breton nationalists, although few in number, were conspicuously active, blowing up a statue in Rennes representing the union of Brittany and France.

The white and black flag (*Gwenn ha du*) regarded today as the Breton standard was created in 1926 by Morvan Marchal, a nationalist, with its symbolic reference back to the medieval days of Breton 'independence'. The hermines are from the duchy's coat of arms and the black bands represent the five bishoprics of Haute Bretagne and the white those of Basse Bretagne.

In the Second World War Brittany was taken over by the Germans in June 1940. About 150,000 soldiers of three army corps came in as the last British troops left, sabotaging the ports as they went. Submarines were soon operating from Brest, Lorient and St-Nazaire, which all became the targets of allied air-raids. Remains of the defensive structures of the Mur de l'Atlantique are still visible around the coast. Many groups of resistance fighters were active in Brittany, often working in conjunction with allied parachutists. A small number of extreme nationalists, like Olier Mordrel, collaborated openly with the enemy. The Museum of the Resistance at St-Marcel in Morbihan presents a vivid picture of these hard times of occupation. Liberation began in July 1944 as the allied forces moved steadily west. Some places, such as Quimper, drove the Germans out themselves.

The terrible destruction of Brest, St-Malo and Lorient led to many years of reconstruction. Nantes had been taken from Brittany by the Vichy government during the war and this was cemented with the creation of the new department of Loire-Atlantique, head of Pays de la Loire in 1957. In 1950, CELIB (Comité d'étude et de liaison des intérêts bretons) was set up to attract investment into Brittany, with car manufacturers and telecommunications companies later established at Rennes, Vannes and Lannion. Today, the food industry is the largest industrial sector, with shipbuilding and other branches of nautical science also important, along with marine and health technology. The region is renowned for its high standards of education, training and research centres.

Brittany remains the main French fishing area, but numbers involved in the industry have gradually dwindled in the last 50 years. Farming, on the other hand, has modernized and expanded to a powerful agricultural lobby in the most prolific vegetable-growing area in France, which also produces a large proportion of the nation's milk, pork and chicken.

Modern Brittany is far from just a quaint setting for all those standing stones and Celtic tales. Yes, it's a rich land of the imagination and a fertile source of oral tradition, but also a complex, diverse and ever-evolving reality, where history gives legend a run for its money and contemporary culture thrives.

Religion

Appreciation of Brittany's distinctive heritage starts with religion. The region has the largest concentration of religious monuments in Europe, and the faith of the people has fuelled much of their history right from the start, particularly in the west where the evidence today is strongest.

The seven Founding Saints of Brittany and the cathedrals associated with them have a particular place in the Breton pantheon. St-Pol (St-Pol-de-Léon), St-Malo, St-Brieuc, St-Samson (Dol-de-Bretagne) and St-Tugdual (Tréguier) were Welsh incomers, while St-Patern (Vannes) and St-Corentin (Quimper) were natives of the peninsula. In medieval times the Tro Breiz was an important pilgrimage around Brittany, which visited each cathedral, a custom that has been revived recently as a religious or walking exercise covering more than 600 km. Tales of miracle-working by the saints, such as driving out dragons, are probably symbolic stories of attempts to put an end to local paganism.

These saints are 'unofficial', never sanctified by the Roman Catholic hierarchy. The legacy of the simple, intimate faith they embody remains today in the extraordinary number of wayside crosses (marking pilgrims' routes), chapels and sacred springs (fontaines) with a saint's statue, where the waters had healing powers. The tradition of pardons, religious processions on saints' days, is still flourishing mainly in the west, when traditional banners are carried and the faithful – or horses, or even inanimate objects – are blessed. The rural nature of these religious practices is clear in traditions such as the butter pardon of St-Herbot, at which cows' tail hairs are still offered.

The different developments of eastern and western Brittany throws up important contrasts – the official church of Rome held sway in the east via the Romans and the Franks, while Basse-Bretagne to the west was converted by hermit-priests of Ireland, Wales and southwest England with their Celtic practices. Place names starting in Plou (parish), Lan and Loc (holy places) reflect the development of this western area. Here, people retained a close and very human relationship with their saints, calling on them for favours and even resorting to 'punishments' like turning statues to face the wall if their demands remained unmet.

The early saints had a greater hold over the hearts and imaginations of the Bretons than any rivals the official Catholic church could produce, although the cult of Mary or Notre Dame is ubiquitous. Her mother, Saint Anne, also has a high profile here – there's a local legend that she came from the Bay of Douarnenez originally, and even brought Jesus on a visit from the Holy Land. The pardon there at Ste-Anne-la-Palud is one of the best attended in Brittany. Her status as the female patron of Brittany has led to an association with medieval ruler Anne de Bretagne, who has strangely acquired a saint-like image in notions of Breton identity.

Christianity never managed to oust the fascination with death common in Celtic cultures, and Death looms graphically in Breton legend and belief. The usual manifestation is Ankou, Death's skeletal assistant, who drives his cart in search of victims. His skull image, sometimes with killing arrow, is portrayed on many ossuaries in Breton church enclosures. The legendary entrance to the underworld was said to be the Yeun Ellez in the marshes of the Monts d'Arrée; where the lonely landscape has given rise to many tales of danger for the unwary traveller.

The mixture of Christian and earlier pagan beliefs and practices Is rife In western Brittany, often to be seen in church decoration, with many examples of decidedly ribald carvings - often very high up inside or in gargoyle form - and strange figures like the horned man in the porch at Brasparts in the Monts d'Arrée. Druids still perform outdoor rituals, and the powerful animism of Celtic religion remains the origin of sacred springs and groves, and even chapels on hill-tops.

Stone stories

The widespread presence of Neolithic monuments in Brittany sparked a multitude of stories in the days before history and archaeology could explain their original context. In the 19th century, the megaliths became anachronistically associated with the Druids, regarded as sites of ritual sacrifices and debauched pagan revelry in popular imagination. Many alignments today still have local names like Druids Cemetery and Druids Row. The stones are also often associated with the *korrigans*, ugly, mischievous and downright dangerous gnomish imps of Breton legend, who were said to live in or around them.

Similarly, legends evolved to explain the very existence of the stones, thought to have been humans originally. So the alignments called The Wedding Party in the Monts d'Arrée were said to be a drunken group of celebrating guests, literally petrified by an angry priest. Elsewhere standing-stones were once girls dancing on the moors who were punished for their levity, or at Carnac, Roman soldiers turned to stone by a saint they were chasing.

Such was the power of superstition over the common people, that Christianized menhirs are common, with a cross or religious engravings added to standing stones – such as the Menhir de St-Uzec near Pleumeur-Bodou in the Lannion area – to reclaim the stones for the Church and turn the tide of pagan practices.

Contents

Footnotes

Menu reader

General

à la carte individually priced menu items
Appellation d'Origine Contrôlée (AOC) label of regulated origin, signifying quality; usually associated with wine, though can also apply to cider and regional foods such as cheeses
biologique/bio organic
carte des vins wine list
déjeuner lunch
dîner dinner or supper
entrée starter
hors d'oeuvre appetizers
menu/formule set menu
petit déjeuner breakfast
plat du jour dish of the day
plat principal main course
une carafe d'eau a carafe of tap water

Drinks *(boissons)*

bière beer (usually bottled)
bouteille bottle
un café/un petit noir coffee (black espresso)
calva (lambig in western Brittany) calvados (apple brandy)
chocolat chaud hot chocolate
cidre cider
un coca Coca-Cola
un (grand) crème a (large) white coffee
dégustation tasting
un demi a measure of beer (33cl)
demi-sec medium-dry – or slightly sweet when referring to Champagne
diabolo menthe mint syrup mixed with lemonade
doux the sweetest Champagne or cider
eau gazeuse/pétillante sparkling/slightly sparkling mineral water
eau plate/minérale still/mineral water
glaçons ice cubes
jus de fruit fruit juice
ker Breton cider and cassis
kir popular apéritif made with white wine and a fruit liqueur
lait milk
une noisette espresso with a dash of milk
orange pressée freshly squeezed orange juice
panaché beer/lemonade shandy

pastis anise-flavoured apéritif
pichet jug, used to serve water, wine or cider
poiré perry (cider made with pears rather than apples)
une pression a glass of draught beer
sec dry
sirop fruit syrup or cordial mixed with still/sparkling water or soda
un thé tea, usually served *nature* with a slice of lemon (*au citron*) – if you want milk ask for *un peu de lait froid*, a little cold milk.
une tisane/infusion herbal tea
un verre de a glass of
un (verre de) vin rouge/blanc/rosé a (glass of) red/white/rosé wine

Fruit *(fruits)* and vegetables *(légumes)*

ail garlic
algues seaweed
ananas pineapple
artichaut artichoke
asperge asparagus
blettes Swiss chard
cassis blackcurrants
céleri-rave celeriac, usually served grated in mayonnaise
cèpes porcini mushrooms
champignons de Paris button mushrooms
châtaignes/marrons chestnuts
choux cabbage
citron lemon
citrouille/potiron pumpkin
courge marrow or squash
épinards spinach
fenouil fennel
fèves broad beans
figues figs
fraises strawberries
framboises raspberries
gratin dauphinois a popular side-dish of potato slices layered with cream, garlic and butter and baked in the oven
haricots cocos small, white beans
haricots verts green beans
lentilles vertes green lentils
mesclun a mixture of young salad leaves
mirabelles small golden plums
myrtilles blueberries/bilberries
noix walnuts
oseille sorrel, often served in a sauce with salmon
pêches peaches
petits pois peas

poireaux leeks
poires pears
pomme de terre potato, *primeurs* are new potatoes (or any early fruit or vegetable), and *frites* are chips (chips are crisps)
pommes apples
prunes plums
salicorne saltwort
soupe au pistou a spring vegetable soup with pistou
truffe truffle

Fish *(poissons)* and seafood *(fruits de mer)*

aiglefin haddock
anchoïade anchovy-based spread
anchois anchovies
anguille eel
araignée spider crab
assiette de fruits de mer plate of shellfish/seafood
bar sea bass (bar de ligne is wild sea bass)
bigorneau winkle
bulots sea snails/whelks
bourride white fish stew, thickened with aïoli
brochet pike
cabillaud cod
calamar/encornet squid
colin hake
coquillage shellfish
coquilles St-Jacques scallops
crevettes prawns/shrimps
dorade sea bream
homard lobster
huîtres oysters
lieu jaune pollack
lotte monkfish
maquereau mackerel
morue salt-cod
moules mussels
oursins sea urchins
palourdes clams
poissons de rivière river fish
poulpe octopus
poutines very tiny, young sardines
rascasse scorpion fish
rouget red mullet
Saint-Pierre John Dory
saumon salmon
soupe de poisson a smooth rockfish-based soup, served with croutons, rouille and grated gruyère cheese
soupions small squid
thon tuna
truite trout

Meat *(viande)* and poultry *(volaille)*

à point medium cooked meat (or tuna steak), usually still pink inside

agneau lamb

andouille/andouillette soft sausage made from pig's small intestines, usually grilled

bien-cuit well-cooked

blanquette de veau veal stew in white sauce with cream, vegetables and mushrooms

bleu barely cooked meat, almost raw

boeuf beef

boucherie butcher's shop or display

canard duck

charcuterie encompasses sausages, hams and cured or salted meats

chevreuil venison, roe deer

confit process to preserve meat, usually duck, goose or pork

cuisse de grenouille frog's leg

daube marinated beef, or sometimes lamb, braised slowly in red wine with vegetables

dinde turkey

escargot snail

faux-filet beef sirloin

foie-gras fattened goose or duck liver

fumé(e) smoked

gigot d'agneau leg of lamb

jambon ham; look for *jambon d'Amboise*, an especially fine ham

lapin rabbit

lièvre hare

médaillon small, round cut of meat or fish

mouton mutton

pavé thickly cut steak

pintade guinea-fowl

porc pork

pot-au-feu slow-cooked beef and vegetable stew

poulet chicken

rillettes a pâté-like preparation of pork belly cooked slowly in pork fat, then shredded; also made with duck, goose, chicken or tuna.

rillons big chunks of pork cooked in pork fat

ris de veau sweetbreads

sanglier wild boar

saucisse small sausage, dried (sèche) or fresh

saucisson large salami-type sausage, for slicing

veau veal

Desserts *(desserts)*

café gourmand selection of desserts with a cup of coffee included

chantilly whipped, sweetened cream

clafoutis dessert of fruit (traditionally cherries) baked in sweet batter, served hot or cold

compôte stewed fruit, often as a purée

crème anglaise thin custard; normally served cold

fromage blanc unsweetened fresh cheese, similar to quark, served on its own or with a fruit coulis – most people add a little sugar

glace ice cream (boules de glace is scoops of ice cream)

coupe glacée cold dessert with ice cream, fruit or nuts, chocolate or chantilly

le parfum flavour, when referring to ice cream or yoghurt

île flottante soft meringue floating on custard, with caramel sauce

liègeois chilled chocolate or coffee ice cream-based dessert topped with chantilly

pâtisserie pastries, cakes and tarts – also the place where they are sold

sabayon creamy dessert made with egg yolks, sugar and wine or liqueur

tarte au citron lemon tart

tarte au pomme apple tart

Other

aïoli garlic mayonnaise

assiette plate (eg *assiette de charcuterie*)

beurre butter

beurre blanc buttery white wine sauce often served with fish

bordelaise red wine sauce served with steak.

boulangerie bakery selling bread and viennoiserie

casse-croûte literally 'to break a crust' – a snack

crêpe large pancake served with various fillings; see also *galette*

croque-monsieur grilled ham and cheese sandwich

croque-madame as above but topped with a fried egg

en croûte literally 'in crust'; food cooked in a pastry parcel

escargots snails

fleur de sel speciality hand-harvested sea salt

forestière generally sautéed with mushrooms

fromage de brebis ewe's milk cheese

fromage de chèvre goat's milk cheese

galette large pancake served with various fillings; see also *crêpe*

garniture garnish, side-dish

gaufre waffle, usually served with chocolate sauce

pan bagnat sandwich version of *salade niçoise*, dressed with lashings of olive oil and vinegar

pâte pastry or dough, not to be confused with *pâtes*, which is pasta or *pâté*, the meat terrine

petits farcis usually small onions, tomatoes, peppers and courgettes stuffed with a mixture of veal, Parmesan and vegetables

pistou a basil and garlic sauce, similar to Italian pesto but without pine nuts or Parmesan/pecorino

riz rice

rouille saffron, garlic and paprika mayonnaise, served with *soupe de poisson* and *bouillabaisse*

salade verte simple green salad with vinaigrette dressing

soupe/potage soup

viennoiserie baked items such as croissants and brioches

Useful phrases

I'd like to reserve a table *Je voudrais réserver une table*

What do you recommend? *Qu'est-ce que vous me conseillez?*

What's the dish of the day? *Qu'est-ce c'est le plat du jour?*

I'd like the set menu *Je vais prendre le menu/la formule*

Does it come with salad? *Est-ce que c'est servi avec de la salade?*

I'd like something to drink *Je voudrais quelque chose à boire*

I'm a vegetarian *Je suis végétarien / végétarienne*

I don't eat... *Je ne mange pas de...*

Where are the toilets? *Où sont les toilettes?*

The bill, please *L'addition, s'il vous plaît*

Index